Scats
and
Tracks
of the

Mid-Atlantic

D1501468

Scats
and
Tracks
of the
Mid-Atlantic

A Field Guide to the Signs of Seventy Wildlife Species

Second Edition

James C. Halfpenny, PhD, and Jim Bruchac
Illustrated by Todd Telander

FALCONGUIDES

GUILFORD, CONNECTICUT

FALCONGUIDES®

An imprint of The Rowman & Littlefield Publishing Group, Inc.
4501 Forbes Blvd., Ste. 200
Lanham, MD 20706
www.rowman.com
Falcon and FalconGuides are registered trademarks and Make Adventure
Your Story is a trademark of The Rowman & Littlefield Publishing Group,
Inc.

Distributed by NATIONAL BOOK NETWORK

Illustrations by Todd Telander

Maps by The Rowman & Littlefield Publishing Group, Inc.

British Library Cataloguing in Publication Information available

Library of Congress Cataloging-in-Publication Data available

ISBN 978-1-4930-4296-8 (paperback)
ISBN 978-1-4930-4297-5 (e-book)

∞™ The paper used in this publication meets the minimum requirements
of American National Standard for Information Sciences—Permanence of
Paper for Printed Library Materials, ANSI/NISO Z39.48-1992.

*To Diann, my alpha partner, ursophile, and tracking
friend, for all her loving support and help.*

JH

*In memory of my grandfather Joseph Bruchac Jr.,
whose feet followed these tracks long before I was born.*

JB

Contents

Acknowledgments

First and foremost, I wish to thank all my students for their years of questions and help, but most of all for the time we've shared tracking and studying in the field. I also wish to thank Lee Fitzhugh; Larry Marlow; Murie Museum; Marty Silver (Warrior's Path State Park, Tennessee) for the times we shared tracking in Tennessee; Teton Science School; and Terry McEneany for his help with bird tracks.

JH

I would like to thank all those that helped with my research, including Melodee James, Eileen Kreiling, Mike Pelton, Bob Sylvester (Catskill Game Farm), Vince Walsh, Ward Stone (New York State Pathologist), Rob DiGiovanni (Senior Biologist River Head Foundation for Marine Research). Jeffrey A. Gottlieb, and April St. Francis (Chief of the Abenaki Nation, Vermont).

JB

Introduction

In the late 1970s, the era of watchable wildlife arrived in the United States. Baby boomers wanted to turn to and experience the outdoors. Television brought wildlife closer than ever. Bird watching thrived. Now more than ever, millions of people want to watch wild animals. Wildlife are not always easy to find and observe, though. Finding tracks and signs is an exciting alternative to actually seeing the animals. Trackable wildlife adds another dimension to the outdoor experience. Jim, Todd, and I wish to share that dimension, the joy of reading stories written in the soil and snow.

Upwards of ten books on tracking have been written in the United States during each decade of the twentieth century. Most are general, covering the United States or all of North America. In *Scats and Tracks of the Mid-Atlantic*, we focus on one biogeographic region, with details about the region's most common or characteristic species of mammals, birds, reptiles, and amphibians. (We have included a few rare species because of their particular interest or significance in a region. For example, what a coup it would be to document a mountain lion, or a fisher, or a red wolf.) We've intentionally limited the number of species covered in order to keep the information manageable. This guide is small, allowing you to carry it in a pack or pocket and use it frequently.

As your knowledge and interest in tracking grows, you may want to find additional information and help. Key references are listed in Selected Reading. For a more detailed investigation of tracking, I recommend my book *A Field Guide to Mammal Tracking in North America* (1986, Johnson Publishing, Boulder, Colorado), and titles by Mark Elbroch, Louise R. Forrest, Louis Liebenberg,

Jim Lowrey, David Moskowitz, Olaus Murie, and Paul Rezendes.

Two organizations will, in computer parlance, provide interactive access to expand your tracking background. A Naturalist's World (ANW), directed by myself, is an ecologically oriented company dedicated to providing educational programs and materials reflecting North America's natural history. Diann Thompson and I run the daily business, teach classes, and lead programs. Our on-site classes provide hands-on experience and in-depth information about animals, their tracks, and the ecology of their environments. In addition to tracking classes, our field programs cover bears, wolves, winter ecology, the northern lights, and alpine ecology. ANW also provides books, videos, slide shows, and computer programs for self-study and as teaching and field aids. You can check out ANW on the Internet at www.tracknature.com. Class schedules, product information, and information about ANW can be obtained from PO Box 989, Gardiner, MT 59030; phone (406) 848–9458.

The Ndakinna Wilderness Project, directed by Jim Bruchac, offers animal tracking classes and adventures for all ages and levels of expertise. Tracking trips venture into the northeastern forest by foot, snowshoe, or canoe. Other topics offered by Ndakinna include natural history, basic wilderness skills, and northeastern native culture. Class schedules and general information can be obtained from 23 Middle Grove Road, Greenfield Center, NY 12833; phone (518) 583–9980, or on the Web at www.ndakinnna.org.

Keep on tracking!

—*James C. Halfpenny*

About tracking

Tracking is for everyone, beginner and expert, young and old. The fun of nature's challenge is solving the mystery written in the trail. Prepare yourself by learning the background and basics of tracking before exercising your skills in the field.

Field notes and preserving tracks

To the natural history detective, the track and trail are things of great beauty and significance. They tell part of the story of an animal's life. Tracks and trails deserve to be preserved, both to increase your knowledge and as a record you can share with others. Preservation is commonly made in the form of written notes, casts, or photographs.

Perhaps the most important item in the naturalist's tool kit is the field notebook. Field notes can jog the memory and facilitate better retention of knowledge. The notes can be analyzed later and can be preserved as records of chance encounters. Writing good field notes is an art form and a science in itself. Field notes are a source of pride when shown to others and may gain recognition for recording rare and unusual events. And need I mention how quickly memories, especially for details, fade when not preserved?

While great and complex systems have been designed for complete and accurate records, there are really but three requirements for the tracker: ruler, paper, and pen. With these, every trail becomes a record for later analysis and sharing. We cannot emphasize enough the importance of enhancing your tracking experience by keeping notes to which you can later refer!

A simple 3-by-5-inch notebook and a 6-inch ruler are adequate to get started. Use a pencil or a pen that won't run if your notes get wet. To facilitate taking notes, A

Naturalist's World produces a waterproof notebook that contains information about footprint groups, gaits, and how to track; data sheets for recording information; and English and metric rulers imprinted on the back cover. See the Introduction for contact information for A Naturalist's World.

Tracks may also be preserved by photographing and making casts. Good photographs can be made by any modern camera that can take a good close-up. When taking pictures, try to fill the viewfinder with the footprint. Get as close as possible. Always include a ruler or some other object in the photo to provide a sense of scale. Avoid using hats, gloves, hands, or objects without a straight edge; round edges do not lend themselves to making accurate measurements from a photo. To avoid distortion, take the photograph from directly above the track, shooting straight down. Also, step back and take photographs of the trail to show the footprints that were photographed close-up. Fast films (ASA of 200 or higher) are generally best, because tracks are often found in dark places, especially ground surfaces. Modern digital cameras take excellent photographs that can easily be e-mailed to others.

Plaster casts are the old standby for preserving tracks. We suggest a casting kit that includes a 1-gallon (4-liter), wide-mouthed plastic jar with a screw lid for carrying dry plaster, a narrow spatula, a plastic mixing cup such as those sold in gas station convenience stores for medium-size drinks, paper for wrapping and transporting the finished cast, and a plastic sack for cleanup. A bottle of water may be needed if water is not available on-site. Two pounds of plaster will make at least four coyote-size track casts.

Purchase plaster from a lumberyard or hardware store, as prices will be more reasonable than at a drugstore or hobby shop. Almost any plaster will work, including plaster of paris, hydrocal, ultracal, or hydrostone. Avoid getting plaster for wallboard or patching compound. These plasters are formulated to be slightly flexible on walls and do not get hard enough for casts.

Two factors are critical to preventing casts from breaking: thickness and density. In the field, thickness is assured by building a wall around the track to contain the plaster. Natural objects such as twigs, stones, and dirt may be used to make a retaining wall 0.25 to 0.5 inch (0.6 to 1.3 cm) above the track. Alternatively, walls in the form of plastic strips cut from milk cartons or other plastic containers may be taken to the field. Proper density is assured by mixing two parts of plaster to one part of water by volume (read instructions on plaster container) to create a mixture similar in consistency to thick pancake batter or a thin milk shake.

Place your spatula close to the track and pour onto the spatula to break the fall of the plaster into the footprint. Working quickly, so the plaster does not set and become too thick, gently pour the plaster first into the fine detailed areas of the footprint and then the rest of the print. Finally, pour the plaster to an appropriate depth (inside the retaining wall) to keep the cast from breaking. Vibrating the spatula up and down across the top of the plaster will cause it to settle evenly and create a smooth back for the cast.

Allow the plaster to dry for 30 minutes, or as long as is recommended on the plaster package. Gently pick the plaster up by digging your fingers under opposite sides of the cast, and turn the cast over onto one hand. Now wash off the dirt by rubbing the cast with your fingertips under the flowing water of a stream or a hose. Do not wash the cast in a sink as plaster may clog the drain. Let the cast continue to cure for several days in a warm, dry environment. If you need to transport it, wrap the cast in paper. Never wrap the cast in plastic as trapped moisture may cause it to crumble.

While special techniques are needed for dust and snow, this procedure will allow casting in many situations. Remember, carry a plastic garbage bag and always clean up your mess. No sign of your plaster should remain to reduce the experience of others who happen by later.

Make Your Own Track Plates

Another method to preserve tracks is to use track plates. A track plate is a surface coated with a material that clings to the animal's feet and leaves a minimum outline print on a collection board. Soot and chalk make good recording materials. (My book, *Track Plates for Mammals: A How-to Manual and Aid to Footprint Identification*, explains the many types and methods of making track plates.)

Make a low-cost, simple track plate box by cutting one end out of a small cardboard box. Fix a piece of clear contact paper sticky side down to the bottom of the box near the opening. Fix a second piece, sticky side up, to the back half using rings of tape. Place bait at the closed end of the box (peanut butter is good bait for many animals).

To record the tracks make a thin paste of carpenter's chalk (purchase at hardware store) mixed with rubbing alcohol and spread it onto the contact paper at the open end. As the alcohol evaporates, the chalk sticks to the paper and the powder will not blow away. The box is now ready.

When the animal walks across the chalk, the powder sticks to its feet. Then when the animal steps on the sticky paper, great prints are recorded. Place a piece of blank paper onto the sticky paper and then remove the two pieces of paper. The clear contact paper will show the footprints and can be placed on a copier to make copies.

Scats and bird pellets

Scats and bird pellets (also called cough pellets or cast-ings) are often helpful for identifying an animal or completing the story written in the trail. Scats and pellets help identify not only what the animal was eating, but who the animal was. However, it should be noted that scats and pellets won't help you identify an animal with as much certainty as tracks will. Many animals make similar scats and pellets that are difficult to tell apart.

The scats of many carnivores are very similar, especially when the diet is mostly meat. Size alone does not provide a definitive answer because of the wide range of diameters produced within a species and even by a single member of a species. For example, fox produce scats ranging in size from 0.3 to 0.8 inch (0.8 to 2.0 cm), coyotes produce scats from 0.5 to 1.3 inches (1.3 to 3.3 cm), and wolves produce scats from 0.5 to 1.5 inches (1.3 to 3.8 cm), and we all know how our own scat varies in size and shape. When judging size, consider both the total quantity of scat and the size of individual pieces. Moist food produces slimmer scats, while fibrous diets produce wider scats.

Given these cautions, scat shapes can be used to identify general groups of animals (see page xix). Spherical shapes flattened top to bottom are deposited by members of the rabbit order. Elongate spheres are deposited by rodents and shrews, and at larger sizes by deer and their relatives. Long, thick cords are deposited by dogs, bears, and raccoons. Dog scats typically have tapered ends, while those from bears and raccoons are blunt. Cats also produce thick cords with blunt ends, but they tend to be constricted or even broken into short segments. Cords that loop back on themselves are produced by members of the weasel family.

Birds, in general, produce long, thin cords or shape-less, semiliquid excretions. Reptiles and amphibians may produce small elongate spheres or long, thin cords. White, nitrogenous urine deposits, found only on the scats of birds, reptiles, and amphibians, separate them from mammal scats.

Scats may be confused with cough pellets. Many bird groups, including owls, raptors, crows, ravens, jays, magpies, gulls, herons, storks, flycatchers, and kingfishers, produce cough pellets in addition to scats. Birds pass digestive juices through what they have eaten to remove the nutrients. Hair, bones, beaks, claws, and other nondigestible parts accumulate in the gizzard (anterior portion of stomach), are compressed, and are coughed up as pellets. Bone and hair remnants in the pellet are easy to identify and tell much about the bird's feeding habits and even the habitats it frequents.

Pellets are grayish in color and are spherical or long and tapered at both ends. When fresh, they are covered

by mucus and appear dark black. Pellets are found mainly at roosting sites and nests, and occasionally at feeding areas. They are deposited singly, but many may accumulate beneath a tree where a bird is roosting, nesting, or perching.

cough pellet

Nitrogenous scat deposits on the ground or twigs may help verify an object as a pellet.

The diameter of the throat determines the maximum diameter of the pellet. In general, large birds produce larger pellets. Shape and diameter allow one to distinguish to some degree between species.

Birds generally produce two pellets per day and regurgitate just before taking flight. The time of day when feeding occurred may affect the sample of food items. For example, owls tend to feed on mammals that come out only at night, while hawks feed on animals that are out during daylight hours.

Shapes of scats

Spheres

Rabbits and their relatives

rabbit

Spheres, elongate

Rodents, shrews, deer, and their relatives

woodrat

shrew

elk

Cords, long and thick

Wolves, bears, raccoons, and their relatives

coyote

bear

raccoon

Cords, thick and often constricted

Mountain lions and their relatives

mountain lion

Cords, often folded

Weasels and their relatives

mink

Cords, long and thin, often with nitrogenous deposits

Birds, reptiles, and amphibians

Canada goose

lizard

Anatomy and footprint nomenclature

The feet of mammals, birds, reptiles, and amphibians are anatomically complex, and that complexity shows in their footprints. Knowing something of the anatomy of their feet will aid in footprint identification and interpreting trails.

The toes of all animals are numbered from the inside of the foot out (the inside of the foot being the side closest to the animal). Therefore, in humans and other mammals, the thumb or big toe (if present) is number 1 and the little finger or little toe is number 5. In birds, toe 1 (if present) points backward.

Over evolutionary time, toes of animals have become reduced in size or have disappeared altogether. In cats and dogs, toe 1 is absent or reduced to a small toe called a dewclaw. In deer, elk, sheep, and similar mammals, toe 1 is absent and toes 2 and 5 are reduced and form dewclaws. Toes 3 and 4, the clouts, form the cloven hoof. In pronghorn antelope, toes 1, 2, and 5 are absent. In birds, toe 5 is absent and toe 1 is often reduced, and occasionally is absent. In the amphibians covered here, toe 1 has been lost from the front foot.

Track measurements

To more accurately determine the animal's foot size from its tracks, mountain lion researchers Fjelline and Mansfield (1989) developed the minimum outline method of measuring tracks.

Place your hand on a hard surface, a table for instance. Note the contact area of your hand with that surface. If your hand went no deeper into that surface, your handprint would have only one size, the minimum outline. If your hand were to sink deeper into the surface as it would if the surface were, say, mud, it would create a series of variable outlines, each larger than the one before, as the mud flowed around the curved surface of your hand. All footprints have a minimum outline, but only prints that sink into a surface have variable outlines.

Note that while the variable outline of a footprint may only be several millimeters wider than the minimum outline, those few millimeters have a large visual effect. The human eye sees area, and area increases with the square of a linear measurement. In short, a few millimeters of width add a lot of area to a footprint.

The minimum outline size does not change for different surfaces, and therefore provides a standard for comparison between surfaces. And though one animal may leave many sizes of footprints depending on surface, slope, and speed, there is only one minimum outline for every footprint that animal might leave. The minimum outline measurement is the only constant and consistent size in tracking.

To measure the minimum outline, study the bottom of a print. The *break point* where the rounded pad turns upward is the edge of the minimum outline. Use this edge to measure tracks.

cross section of footprint in ground

Assigning the break point is a subjective judgment and no two people will always mark it at exactly the same point. However, testing has shown that an individual tracker using the minimum outline method can reduce personal variation in measurement and that groups of trackers using this method will also become more consistent in their measurement of tracks. Remember the computer rule GIGO: garbage in, garbage out. You cannot get quality measurements from a bad track. Quality measurements are the tracker's goal, and using minimum outline methods greatly reduces overexaggeration and variance in measurement.

All measurements in this guide are minimum outline measurements.

The measurements in *Scats and Tracks of the Mid-Atlantic* are mostly averages gathered from years of tracking. Averages include only animals judged to be adult. Length is measured parallel and width is measured perpendicular to the foot axis. However, it is important to remember the great size variation among animals. Every animal was small once in its life, and some never get big. Males are often substantially larger than females. Regional variations in mammal sizes also occur. For example, coyotes are smaller in the southwestern United States and larger in the northeastern part of the country. Their tracks vary accordingly. Therefore, a track in the field may be considerably larger or smaller than the measurements provided. Use track measurements only as a rough guideline, not as an absolute rule. Collect your own database of track measurements for your area.

Gaits and trails

Coordinated muscle movements result in the various gaits used by animals. In the simplest form, when moving on two legs (bipedal movement), an organism can walk, run, and hop. When moving on four legs (quadrupedal movement), an organism can walk, trot, lope, gallop, bound, and pronk (also called stot). Though other gaits exist, we will confine our discussion to these basic gaits. Each gait leaves a characteristic pattern that may be modified by changes in speed and body angle. The combination of footprints is called the trail. The bipedal walk and run and the quadrupedal walk and trot result in gaits that are *symmetrical.* The right side of the trail is a mirror image of the left side. The trail patterns for these gaits are the same, alternating right-left pattern, and they differ only by the stride being longer in the run and trot than it is in the walk. In the run and trot, the straddle, the distance from the right edge of the rightmost pad (see page xxvii) to the left edge of the leftmost pad, also tends to be narrower than it is in the walk.

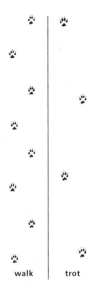

walk   trot

Quadrupedal movement results in gaits that are *asymmetrical* (the right half of the trail is not always a mirror image of the left), including lope, gallop, bound, hop, and pronk. These gaits produce patterns that include all four footprints (two fronts, two hinds, two rights, and two lefts) in a group separated from the next group by a space where no footprints appear.

In *gallops,* the feet, front and rear, that move first (or *lead*) will determine whether the gallop will form a Z-shaped or C-shaped pattern. When the front and hind feet on the same side lead, the pattern takes on a Z shape. A right front lead, with a left hind lead, or vice versa, results in a C-shaped pattern. Thus, there are four possible gallop patterns.

C-shaped gallop   Z-shaped gallop

large print–front feet
small print–rear feet

Bounds (also known as hops and jumps) are characterized by the synchronization of the hind feet; both strike the ground at the same time, side by side. The front feet strike the ground at a different time than the hind feet. In a full bound, the front feet are synchronized and strike the ground side by side at the same time. In a half bound, only the hind feet are synchronized and the front feet hit the ground staggered. Animals that mostly use full bounds, also called hops, live in trees (tree squirrels and songbirds), whereas those that mostly use half bounds live on the ground (ground squirrels, rabbits, and grouse).

In a *pronk* (also called a *stot*), all four feet strike the ground at the same time, with the front feet side by side and forward of the hind feet, which are also side by side. This gait is often used by deer to gain height and increase time in the air to look around.

To increase peripheral vision, non-primate mammals have eyes placed toward the sides of their head, not flat on their face like humans. By turning sideways, a prey species can see what is pursuing it and where it needs to go to escape. The predator, by turning sideways, can see what it is chasing and where the rest of the predator pack is.

Consequently, quadrupedal mammals have evolved to use all gaits while their body is turned to the side. These *side gaits* result when the animal's heavy head deviates from the line of travel and the body turns sideways. First, the front feet respond by moving toward the side of the trail where the head is. Then, as the head turns more, the hind feet move to the side away from the head. The greater the head movement, the greater the angle of the side gait. Common examples are the side trot and side gallop, which are often used by canids. These are often called a dog trot or dog gallop.

An animal's size is also reflected in its gait patterns. When a mammal is walking with its normal gait, for example, the stride is 1.1 to 1.25 times larger than the distance from the hip to the shoulder joint. Using this crude relationship, body size can be judged from a walking stride. A 22-inch stride indicates a hip-to-shoulder length of 20 inches. Add to the hip-to-shoulder distance an estimate for the head length beyond the shoulder joint and an estimate of the rump length beyond the hip joint to get a total estimate of animal body length.

Speed also modifies gait patterns in trails. There are three rules governing how pattern changes as speed changes.

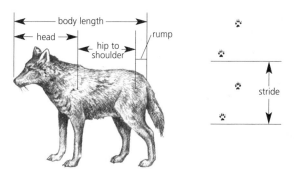

estimating mammal length from stride

1. As speed increases, the hind foot lands farther forward than the front footprint on the same side. Conversely, as speed decreases, the hind foot lands farther back in relation to the front footprint.

2. As speed increases, stride increases.

3. As speed increases, straddle usually decreases.

Speed changes are easily observed in quadrupedal walk and trot trail patterns. As speed increases, the hind footprint registers in front of the front print. This faster version of a walk is called an amble. The faster version of a trot doesn't have a name. When the animal slows to the point that the hind feet are registering behind the front prints, the animal may be stalking something. Trots are separated from walks by having a stride two or more times greater than the estimated hip-to-shoulder distance of an animal.

A slow version of the gallop is also recognizable. When a gallop slows to the point that one or more hind feet register behind the leading edge of the frontmost footprint in a group pattern, the gait is called a *lope*. The gait is still a gallop, it's just a slow gallop.

Trail measurements

The terms stride, group, intergroup, and straddle describe the size of an animal trail. The stride is measured from the point where a foot touches the ground surface to where the same point of the same foot next touches the surface, and consists of one group and one intergroup measurement. The group consists of all four footprints (two fronts, two hinds, two lefts, two rights), while the *intergroup* is the distance between groups. Gait patterns take their name from the configuration of the group. The stride provides an indication of size in a walking animal and an indication of relative speed for other gaits (see pages xxiii and xxiv).

walk (slower) | amble (faster)

1 x 2 x 1 lope | 2 x 2 lope | 3 x 3 lope

The *straddle* indicates the width of the trail and is measured from the outside rightmost pad of the outside right footprint of a group to the outside leftmost pad footprint of the same group. The outside edges of the trail are used because the inside of footprints overlap for many carnivore species. When measured from outside right to outside left, walking straddle is an indicator of size.

Stride, group, and intergroup are all measured parallel to the trail, while the straddle is measured at right angles to the trail. Select a straight section of trail on level ground to measure. The slightest curve in the trail will distort the straddle measurement.

Glossary of terms

amble: a fast walk in which the hind footprint registers anterior to the front footprint. See illustration on page xxvi.

asymmetrical: not symmetrical, that is, one side is not a mirror image of the opposite side.

bound: a gait in which both hind feet strike the ground at the same time, side by side. If the front feet also land side by side, the motion is said to be a *full bound*. A *half bound* occurs when one front foot strikes the ground in front of the other. See illustration on page xxiii.

clout: term used to refer to toe 3 or toe 4 of the hoof. See illustration on page xxxii.

convergent toes: toes 2 and 4 of ducks, geese, and swans, which bend toward the foot axis, especially at the tips. Compare to *divergent* toes.

cord: See s*cat shape*.

cough pellet: remnants of bones and hair coughed up by many bird species after feeding on prey.

dewclaw: toe that over evolutionary time has become reduced in size and raised on the leg, away from the other toes. For example, toe 1 in dogs and toes 2 and 5 in deer.

diagnostic: providing certain identification of an animal or its sign.

digitigrade: walking on the tips of the toes. Dogs and cats, for example, are digitigrade. Tracks left by digitigrade animals rarely show a sole. Compare *plantigrade*.

digit: one of the toes of an animal.

digital pad: See *pad*.

distal webbing: See *webbing*.

divergent toes: Toes that are straight or turn out from the foot axis at the tips, specifically toes 2 and 4 of sea gulls. Compare to *convergent* toes.

foot axis: imaginary line down the center of the foot. It runs between toes 3 and 4 in deer and their relatives, and down toe 3 of other mammals. In birds, the foot axis also runs down toe 3.

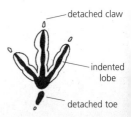

detached claw

indented lobe

detached toe

fringe: webbing attached to a single toe. May have a smooth edge, known as a *simple fringe* or *simple lobe*, or it may be wavy, in which case it is said to have *indented lobes*.

full bound: See *bound*.

gait: term for the type(s) of movement an animal uses when moving. Examples of gaits include *walk, amble, trot, bound,* and *gallop*. Gaits are defined by the mechanics of body movement, not by speed.

gallop: a gait in which hind feet move around the front feet and (usually) strike the ground in front of the front feet. Galloping forms distinct group patterns (two fronts, two hinds, two lefts, two rights) separated by an intergroup distance from the next set of four feet. Gallops fall into two basic patterns: Z-shaped and C-shaped.

group: a subunit of a *stride* including four footprints (two fronts and two hinds, and two lefts and two rights). The measure of the group plus the intergroup equals the measure of the stride.

half bound: See *bound*.

heel: portion of foot or track to the rear of digital and interdigital pads. In mammals,

gallops   **bounds**

may be covered with hair, naked (without hair), or have one or more proximal pads. In reptiles and amphibians, may be textured with *tubercles*.

hop: synonymous with *bound*, often used in reference to *gaits* of rodents and rabbits.

indented lobe: See *fringe*.

interdigital pad: See *pad*.

length: of a track, the distance from front of toe *pads* to back of the interdigital pads, measured parallel to the *foot axis*. In mammal tracks, does not include claws. In bird tracks, does not include toe 1, but includes claws if they are attached and indistinguishable from toe pad.

line of travel: imaginary line on the ground over which the center of gravity of an animal passes.

lobe: See *fringe*.

lope: a slow *gallop*, in which at least one hind foot registers behind a front foot in a group of four footprints. See illustration on page xxvi.

mesial webbing: See *webbing*.

minimum outline: See pages xx and xxi for extended discussion.

nipple-dimple: See *scat shape*.

outer toe angle: in birds, the angle between toes 2 and 4. In perching birds less than 90 degrees and in shorebirds greater than 120 degrees.

oval: See *scat shape*.

pad: hard, calluslike structure on the sole of an animal's foot. Each toe may have a digital pad. One or more interdigital pads are located directly to the rear of the toes, and one or more proximal pads may be located directly to the rear of the interdigital pads. In deer and their relatives, there is a single pad separated from the *wall* by the *subunguis*. In birds, a metatarsal pad may occur directly under the leg bone.

plantigrade: walking on the soles of the foot. Raccoons, bears, and humans, for example, are plantigrade. The sole of the foot usually shows in the footprint. Compare *digitigrade*.

pronk: a *gait* in which all four feet strike the ground simultaneously and directly below the body. The group pattern shows two front footprints ahead of the two hind prints. Also called a *stot*. See illustration on page xxiv.

proximal pad: See *pad*.

proximal webbing: See *webbing*.

rotatory gallop: a type of *gallop* that tends to form a C-shaped *group* pattern. See illustration on page xxiii.

run: a *gait* used when moving only on two legs. It differs from a *walk* in having a longer *stride*.

scat shape: *Cords* are long pieces of scat, typically four to ten times longer than the width. Ends may be blunt or tapered. *Ovals* are pieces of scat typically two to four times longer than wide and tapered at both ends. A *nipple-dimple*-shaped scat pellet has a point at one end and a depression at the other. See chart on page xix.

simple fringe, simple lobe: See *fringe*.

sole: bottom of an animal's foot. It may be covered with hair or naked, and may have one or more *pads* on it.

stot: See *pronk*.

straddle: the distance from the right edge of the rightmost pad to the leftmost edge of the leftmost pad in a *trail*. Measured at right angles to the *line of travel*.

stride: the distance from the point where a foot touches the ground to the point where the same foot touches the ground again. Measured parallel to the *line of travel*. One stride is equal to a *group* plus an intergroup measurement.

subunguis: the soft material under the nails of humans. In deer and their relatives, refers specifically to the soft material between the *pad* and *wall*. Sometimes misspelled as subunguinis.

symmetrical: having two sides, one the mirror image of the other side.

toe pad: See *pad*.

track: refers to an individual footprint. Some measurable characteristics include *length* and *width*.

track pattern: the gross visual image of the pattern of footprints on the ground. A repeating pattern of two prints separated from the next two is called two-by-two and written 2 x 2. Prints may also show patterns of 3 x 3, 4 x 4, and 1 x 2 x 1. These patterns are made during a *gallop* or a *bound*. A few of these patterns are illustrated on pages xxiii–xxiv.

trail: a series of footprints and associated signs that marks the passage of an animal. Some measurable characteristics include *stride* and *straddle*.

transverse gallop: a type of gallop that tends to form a Z-shaped group pattern. See illustration on page xxiii.

trot: a *gait* in which evenly spaced footprints alternate on right and left sides of the *line of travel*. Front leg moves in diagonal synchronization with opposite hind leg. Hind footprint registers on top of front. As speed increases, hind moves forward of front. Same patterns as a walk, but longer stride. May be done with body turned to side.

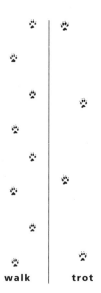

straddle

stride

walk   **trot**

tubercle: rough pinhead-sized protuberance on the sole of the foot of a reptile or amphibian.

unguis: hard material forming nails in humans, hoof walls in deer and their relatives, and claws in other mammals. Composed of hair pasted together by body glues. Sometimes misspelled unguinis.

walk: a *gait* where evenly spaced footprints alternate on right and left sides of the *line of travel*. Hind footprint registers on top of front. As speed increases, hind moves forward of front. See illustrations on pages xxii and xxvi.

wall: hard material around the edge of each clout of a hoof. Technically the unguis, which also forms human nails and animal claws.

webbing: thin membrane stretched between toes of animals. The webbing may be near the tips of the toes (*distal*), about midway to the toe tips (*mesial*), or attached at the base (*proximal*). A membrane attached to only one toe is called a *fringe*.

width: of a *track,* the greatest distance from the right side of the pads of a foot to the left side, whether the greatest distance is across the toes or palm pads. Measured perpendicular to the *foot axis.* In bird tracks, includes claws if they are attached and indistinguishable from toe pad.

How to use *Scats and Tracks*

Scats and Tracks of the Mid-Atlantic is designed for easy use in the field. The gray bars found on the edges of the pages of the track accounts will help you measure scat diameter and footprint size; each of these bars is keyed to the average size of the sign in question. A ruler is provided on the back cover. Below, we provide the background knowledge that every tracker should be familiar with before going to the field or using this book. Please take some time to study this material.

Illustrations

Illustrator Todd Telander applied his great ability to our collections of plaster casts, photographs, and slides, drawing on our experience to produce the most up-to-date and accurate illustrations possible. These drawings made from the best specimens in a collection of thousands represent the culmination of decades of tracking experience and are far more accurate than the tracker usually finds in tracking books. The tracks you find on the ground may not have as much detail or be as clear, but it is better to have an excellent drawing to compare to an imperfect track than to have to compare a track to a drawing lacking critical details.

How to use the track accounts

The track accounts in this guide have been grouped by similar footprint characteristics. Each track account represents a single species or a group of species with similar track characteristics. Each account is presented across a two-page spread, and is conveniently divided into sections as discussed below.

Each account shows a comon and a scientific name. Scientific names in paranthesis indicate older names that have been replaced by taxonomists. Below that is a brief listing of visual characteristics used to identify an animal. These descriptions are general, and great variability of pattern can exist among animals in the field. We recommend consulting appropriate field identification guides.

Track: A concise description of key points of footprints, to be used for identification. The accompanying track illustrations are not at actual size, but, unless otherwise noted, actual (average) length of the footprint is shown as a bar on the right side of the right-hand page. Average width is shown as a bar on the bottom of the right-hand page. In the field, place the appropriate measurement bar next to the track to compare size. To take a numerical measurement, use the ruler printed on the back cover of the book.

The tracks illustrated are all from right feet, except in the entries for birds, where both feet are pictured. Numerical measurements are given in the form *length x width*. Note that measurements of mammal tracks do not include claws, that measurements of bird tracks include claws but do not include toe 1, and that measurements generally do not include parts of the foot that often do not register in a given species's track (e.g., heels in the hind feet of some rodent species).

Trail: The average size of the stride of the most commonly used gait or gaits is given. Other common or characteristic gaits, if any, are discussed. See *track patterns* in the Glossary of Terms on page xxxi. For more information on gaits in tracking, see *A Field Guide to Mammal Tracking in North America* by Jim Halfpenny (1986). Gaits are displayed up the right side of the right-hand page. If the common gait is a walk or trot, however, it may not be illustrated, since all walking and trotting patterns consist of right-left alternating patterns.

Scat: A description of scat supplements the drawing. Average scat width is shown as a bar up the side of the left-hand page. In the field, place the appropriate measurement bar next to the scat to compare size. To take a numerical measurement, use the ruler printed on the back cover of the book. Numerical measurements of scat are given under the illustrations in the form *length x width*. In cases of small scat, only width is given; thus, a single measurement always indicates diameter.

Habitat: To aid in locating and differentiating tracks, the animal's habitat preferences are listed. Some animals with large ranges, such as the beaver, are only found in specific habitats.

Similar species: Clues are provided to help differentiate an animal's tracks from similar tracks of other species. With these clues, identification should be possible.

Other sign: Other sign of animals, besides tracks and scat, are listed or illustrated to help with identification, and simply to provide more information on animal lives.

In addition, a distribution map is provided with each account. This gives a generalized picture of where along the Mid-Atlantic coast an animal may be found. Animals may move outside their common range. Animals that require specific habitats will of course not be evenly distributed through the shown range.

To make the best use of this guide, carry it with you into the field. When you come across an unfamiliar track or trail, open the book to the appropriate track account and place the page alongside the track for immediate on-site comparison.

Visual key to tracks

This simple key includes birds, reptiles, amphibians, and mammals. It is arranged by the number of toes that show in a good footprint, ranging from no toes to two toes to five toes. Those animals that show four toes in the front print and five toes in the hind are listed between four- and five-toed animals.

Fiddler and Horseshoe Crabs (pp. 2–5)

Two to several parallel series of holes in the ground. Trail may be 1 to 12 inches (2.5 to 30 cm) wide and include shell drag marks.

Snakes (pp. 28–29)

Series of side-to-side trail undulations.

Deer and Relatives (pp. 138–41)

Two toes form hard, cloven hoof. Dewclaws may show in deep print.

Birds with Webbed Feet (pp. 30–35, 40–41, 44–47, 62–65)

Three toes facing forward, often a fourth toe facing backward. Claws may be detached from toes. Webbing between two or more toes.

Birds without Webbed Feet (pp. 36–39, 42–43, 48–61, 66–75)

Three toes facing forward, often a fourth toe facing backward. Claws may be detached from toes.

Coyotes, Dogs, and Relatives (pp. 80–87)

Four toes in front and hind prints. Claws usually present and detached. Single anterior lobe on inter-digital pad.

Mountain Lions (Cougars), Bobcats, and Relatives (pp. 88–91)

Four toes in front and hind prints. Claws usually absent. Double anterior lobe on interdigital pad.

Rabbits (pp. 108–11)

Four toes in front and hind footprint. An exceptionally clear print may show a fifth inner toe in the front footprint. Pads lacking, bottom of foot covered with hair. Long hopping heel in hind print.

Salamanders (pp. 8–9)

Four toes in front print, five toes in hind. Trail wide, often with a tail drag.

Frogs (pp. 12–17)

Four toes in front print, five toes in hind. Long, slender toes. Front print faces center of trail. Distal or proximal webbing in hind print.

Toads (pp. 10–11)

Four toes in front print, five toes in hind. Front print faces center of trail. Mesial webbing in hind print. Tubercles may show on front and hind prints.

Rodents (pp. 112–37)

Most have four toes in front prints and five in hind. Beaver has five toes in front print. Front toes show a 1-2-1 grouping, hind show a 1-3-1 grouping. Long hopping heel in hind print.

Lizards (pp. 18–19, 26–27)

Five toes in front and hind prints. Toes long and slender. Claws may be detached. Tail drag often present in trail.

Turtles (pp. 20–25)

Five toes show in front tracks and hind tracks. Front prints toe in and hind prints may toe out. Feet are relatively broad. Claws robust and often visible. Sometimes the claws are the only visible signs on hard ground.

Opossum (pp. 76–77)

Five toes. Distinct hind print with an opposable (like human thumb) inside toe protruding sideways from other toes. Outside toe is slightly separated from middle three toes.

Shrews (pp. 78–79)

Five slender toes present on front and hind feet. In clear prints, four interdigital and two proximal pads may be seen.

Raccoons and Relatives (pp. 94–95)

Five toes in front and hind prints. Toes often round or bulbous at ends. May have long, slender toes.

Weasels and Relatives (pp. 96–107)

Five toes in front and hind prints, though the little toe (on inside of foot) may not show. Toes in a 1-3-1 grouping. Interdigital pad is chevron-shaped. Plantigrade hind foot.

Black Bear (pp. 92–93)

Five toes in front and hind prints, though the little toe (on inside of foot) may not show. Toes evenly spaced. Plantigrade hind foot.

Scats
and
Tracks
of the
Mid-Atlantic

Fiddler Crab
Uca pugilator

Small crab with squarish
shell that tapers at
back and lacks notch
on edge. Eye stalk
longer than space between
eyes. Males have one large
claw, females two small claws.

Track: Each foot creates a simple small hole, which in very wet sand may be slightly elongated.

Trail: Series of roundish holes in roughly parallel lines. Stride varies from 0.1 to 0.3 inches (0.3 to 0.8 cm). Straddle varies from 0.75 to 1.0 inch (1.8 to 2.5 cm). Because the crab moves sideways, its eight feet create four lines of holes but as the crab turns, the number of lines increases up to eight lines.

Scat: Not known.

hole in sand with tracks

Habitat: Sand beaches to muddy beaches for similar species. Burrows in area between tide marks.

Similar species: Footprint holes of ghost crabs usually elongate and they leave wider trails, about 4.0 inches (10.0 cm). Parallel rows of dot-like tracks separate fiddler trails from all other species.

Other sign: Domed entrances to burrows and balls of sand excavated from the burrow.

sideways movement

.75–1.0"

trail

Horseshoe Crab
Limulus polyphemus

Unmistakable hard
horseshoe-shaped shell
with tail spike. May reach
24.0 inches (61.0 cm) in length.
Not a crab but a relative of spiders.

Track: Walking footprints consisting of two elongate holes about 0.75 inch (1.9 cm) wide form an inverted "V." Rarely small hind feet register and look like ski pole baskets.

Trail: A wide, 10.0- to 12.0-inch (25.0- to 30.0-cm) drag mark through the sand consisting of two parallel rows of foot holes inside the shell drag mark. Distance between holes is about 2.0 inches (5.0 cm). Tail drags down the middle of the trail.

Scat: Not known.

egg mass on sandy beach

Habitat: Intertidal to subtidal zones.

Similar species: Broad trail with footprint and trail drag is distinctive from other species.

Other sign: Series of round nest mounds where round, green eggs are deposited. Eggs occasionally exposed by water.

tracks
0.25 x 0.75 in
0.6 x 1.9 cm

Eastern Newt—Red Eft phase
Notophthalmus viridescens

Vienna sausage–size salamander, up
to 4.0 inches (10.0 cm)
long. Moist, smooth
skin. Terrestrial form,
called red eft, is bright
orange-red with red spots outlined in black. Tubercles on
underside of foot.

Track: Four toes on front foot (often only three show), and five
toes on hind foot. The outline of the foot
may not show, just toe prints. Even in a
clear print, tubercles rarely show.

Trail: Walking stride is about 1.0 inch
(2.5 cm). Trail has a wide straddle (0.67
inches [1.6 cm]) relative to stride, and may
show oscillating belly and tail drag marks.

Scat: Brown to black with slightly tapered
ends.

Habitat: Quiet waters around lakes, ponds, and streams in grassland meadow areas and forests.

scat
0.2 x 0.1 in
0.6 x 0.3 cm

SCAT WIDTH

Similar species: Differs from lizards by wider, oscillating tail drag (if present) and by having only four toes on front foot. Considerably smaller tracks and trail than most salamanders.

Other sign: Egg mass found in water along shore.

front
0.2 x 0.2 in
0.5 x 0.5 cm

hind
0.2 x 0.1 in
0.6 x 0.3 cm

slow walk

FRONT TRACK LENGTH

FRONT TRACK WIDTH

Tiger and Spotted Salamander
Ambystoma tigrinum and *A. maculatum*

Hot dog–size salamander, up to 9.0 inches (23.0 cm) long. Moist, smooth skin. Body brown to black to dark green, with yellow spots or streaks. Tubercles on underside of foot.

Spotted salamander
A. maculatum

Track: Four toes on front foot (often only three show), and five toes on hind foot. The outline of the foot may not show, just toe prints. Even in a clear print, tubercles rarely show.

Trail: Walking stride is about 3.0 inches (7.5 cm). Trail has a wide straddle relative to stride, and may show oscillating belly and tail drag marks.

Scat: Soft, pea-size black masses with some hint of oval shape.

scat
0.3 x 0.4 in
0.7 x 0.6 cm

egg mass

Habitat: Quiet waters around lakes, ponds, and streams in grassland meadow areas and forests.

Similar species: Differs from lizards by wider, oscillating tail drag and by having only four toes on front foot. Larger tracks and trail than newts.

Other sign: Eggs in egg masses are attached individually to underwater plant stems.

front
0.6 x 0.3 in
1.5 x 0.8 cm

hind
0.8 x 0.6 in
2.0 x 1.5 cm

**slow
walk**

FRONT TRACK LENGTH

FRONT TRACK WIDTH

American Toad
Anaxyrus (Bufo) americanus

Baseball-size toad, up to
3.5 inches (9.0 cm) long.
Body is plain brown to gray
to reddish, with warts from
yellow to red located in dark
brown or black spots. A white line
runs down the back. Only one or two large warts in each
dark spot. Female larger than male.

Track: Four toes on front foot and five on hind. Front feet face in. Two tubercles on heel of front foot. Three hind toes face in, one forward, and one out. Two tubercles may show on the heel of the hind foot, and can be confused with toes. Webbing, found only on hind feet, extends at most halfway out to toe tips.

Trail: Hopping or full bound stride generally 5.0 to 7.0 inches (13.0 to 18.0 cm). Walking stride is about 2.5 inches (7.5 cm).

scat
0.9 x 0.2 in
2.3 x 0.5 cm

egg mass

toad imprint in mud

SCAT WIDTH

Scat: Dark brown to black. Long cord, up to five times longer than wide. Sometimes contains insect parts.

Habitat: Lake, ponds, beaver ponds, and wet mixed coniferous forest.

Similar species: Differs from frogs by presence of tubercles on front heels. Hind foot is narrower than frog. Walks and uses short hops more than the usually long-hopping frog.

Other sign: Long strings of egg masses on bottom of water source and floating among vegetation.

walk

front
0.8 x 0.5 in
2.0 x 1.3 cm

mesial web

hind
1.0 x 0.9 in
2.5 x 2.3 cm

hop

Chorus Frog
Pseudacris triseriata

Silver dollar–size frog less than 1.5 inches (3.8 cm). Highly variable frog with body color from brown to green. Darker stripe pattern varies with subspecies.

Track: Four toes on front foot and five on hind. Front feet face in. Four hind toes face in, with one facing out. Proximal webbing on hind feet extending at most one-quarter of way out to toe tips.

Trail: Hopping stride about 10.0 inches (25.0 cm). Frogs may easily hop 3.0 feet (1.0 m) when in a hurry.

scat
0.5 x 0.1 in
1.3 x 0.3 cm

egg mass and tadpole

SCAT WIDTH

Scat: Black, firm cord with slightly tapering ends.

Habitat: Shallow water with emergent vegetation including pond and lake shores, marshes, and beaver ponds.

Similar species: Lack the palm tubercles of the front feet of toad. Less webbing between toes. Hop more and longer distances. Smaller than leopard frog.

Other sign: Inconspicuous egg masses consisting of a few eggs in a packet attached to vegetation below waterline.

front
0.6 x 0.4 in
1.5 x 1.0 cm

walk

proximal web

hind
0.8 x 0.6 in
2.0 x 1.5 cm

hop

FRONT TRACK LENGTH

FRONT TRACK WIDTH

Leopard Frog
Lithobates sphenocephalus (Rana utricularia)

Baseball-size frog, 3.5 inches (9.0 cm) long. Body light to dark brown or green, with dark spots. Spots have light borders. Head relatively long and pointed. White stripe on jaw. Often a light spot on eardrum.

Track: Four toes on front foot and five on hind. Front feet face in. Four hind toes face in, with one facing out. Webbing, found only on hind feet, is distal, extending most of the way out to toe tips. Front toe 1 is thick on male, because it serves as the nuptial pad for grasping female during mating.

Trail: Full bound or hopping stride is about 20.0 inches (50.0 cm). May easily hop 3.0 ft (1.0 m) when in a hurry. Occasionally walk.

Scat: Brown to black, with slightly tapered ends.

Habitat: Cold, nonseasonal ponds, streams, and other water sources. May be found in meadows well away from water.

scat
1.5 x 0.4 in
3.8 x 1.0 cm

egg mass

SCAT WIDTH

Similar species: Nuptial pad (enlarged pad for holding female during mating) separates male from other hopping amphibians. Differs from toads by more webbing between toes, lack of palm tubercles on front feet, and by hopping more and at longer distances. Larger than chorus frogs.

Other sign: Softball-size egg masses floating just below water surface.

walk

front
0.8 x 0.6 in
2.0 x 1.5 cm

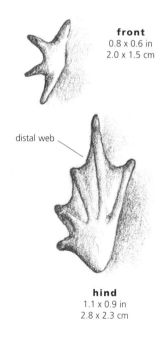

distal web

hind
1.1 x 0.9 in
2.8 x 2.3 cm

hop

FRONT TRACK LENGTH

FRONT TRACK WIDTH

Bullfrog
Lithobates (Rana) catesbeiana

Softball-size frog, 4.0 to 8.0 inches (10.0 to 20.0 cm) long. Brownish-green to green, becoming light green on head. Legs banded with dark brown to green; small spots on back. Fold of skin around eye and large exposed eardrum.

Track: Four toes on front foot and five on hind. Front feet face in. Three hind toes face in, remaining two face forward or out. Webbing, found only on hind feet, is distal, extending most of the way out to the toe tips. In a clear track, a male's toe 2 (thumb) on front foot appears thicker at base.

Trail: Hopping stride is 24.0 inches (60.0 cm). May easily hop 72.0 inches (180.0 cm).

scat
1.5 x 0.4 in
3.8 x 1.0 cm

egg mass

SCAT WIDTH

Scat: Brown to black, with slightly tapered ends.

Habitat: Permanent and (usually) quiet water with dense growth of aquatic plants, especially cattails, in plains, woodlands, and forest.

Similar species: Differs from toads by more webbing between toes, lack of palm tubercles on front feet, and by hopping more and at longer distances. Differs from leopard frog and chorus frog by larger feet.

Other sign: Deposits a globular egg mass.

front
1.5 x 1.0 in
3.8 x 2.5 cm

walk

distal web

hind
1.8 x 0.9 in
4.5 x 2.3 cm

hop

FRONT TRACK LENGTH

FRONT TRACK WIDTH

Alligator
Alligator mississippiensis

Roughly the size of a short telephone pole, body varying from 5.0 to 15.0 feet or more (1.5 to 4.5 m), with dry skin and ridged scales. Black to dark gray body. Broad rounded snout distinguishes it from a crocodile.

Track: Five toes on front foot. Inside and outside toes are opposite and form a straight line. Four toes on hind foot with a well-developed heel. Claws detached. Skin tubercles may show in the bottom of the tracks. Track size varies considerably because alligators continue to grow their entire life.

Trail: Walking stride is about 40.0 inches (100.0 cm), but this varies with alligator size.

Scat: We have not observed their scat.

Habitat: Prefers river swamps, marshes, and bayous.

Similar species: No similar tracks for adults. Young might be confused with turtles, but have four toes on hind feet.

Other sign: Nest composed of vegetation and may be up to 7.0 feet (2.1 m) in diameter and 3.0 feet (90.0 cm) high.

front
about 6.75 x 8.0 in
about 17.0 x 20.0 cm

hind
about 11.0 x 9.0 in
about 28.0 x 23.0 cm

FRONT TRACK LENGTH (50%)

FRONT TRACK WIDTH (40%)

Painted Turtle
Chrysemys picta

A small turtle with
smooth, unkeeled
shells and patterns of
red, yellow, and black.
Length to 8.0 inches
(20.0 cm). Females larger
than males.

Track: Five toes with claws show in
front and back prints. Claws longer on
front feet and those of the male front
feet are two to three times longer than
the female's. Outer toe on hind foot
lacks claw. Distal webbing on front
and hind prints.

Trail: Walking stride averages 4.5
inches (11.5 cm) with a straddle of 4.0
inches (10.0 cm). Front feet toe in and
hind feet toe out. Hind footprint registers slightly behind. Tail drag
often visible.

Scat: Usually black semiliquid, slightly elongated clumps.

scat
0.9 x 0.2 in
1.3 x 0.5 cm

SCAT WIDTH

Habitat: Ponds, lakes, marshes, swamps, streams, and ditches with abundant vegetation.

Similar species: Differs from snapping turtles by its narrow straight trail and by only four claws on hind foot.

Other sign: Nests are usually dug in sand in open areas where sun warms eggs.

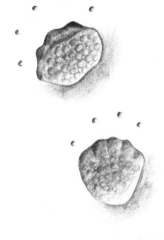

front
0.8 x 0.7 in without claws
2.0 x 1.8 cm

hind
1.1 x 1.0 in without claws
2.8 x 2.5 cm

FRONT TRACK LENGTH

FRONT TRACK WIDTH

Snapping Turtle
Chelydra serpentina

A large to very large turtle,
average weight 10.0
to 30.0 pounds
(4.5 to 16.0
kg). The robust
shell is lined by three
toothed ridges. Large head
with robust, hooked jaw. Tail
longer than half the shell and toothed on top.

Track: Five toes show in front and hind tracks. Front prints toe in and hind prints may toe out. Feet are relatively broad. Claws robust and often visible. Sometimes the claws are the only visible signs on hard ground.

Trail: Walking stride ranges from 5.0 to 12.0 inches (12.5 to 30.0 cm). Straddle is wide compared to stride. Tail drag often present.

Scat: Lacks well-defined shape. Color is algae-green to dark black. Often soft.

Habitat: Always near water, including swamps, marshes, lakes, streams, and rivers.

scat
1.5 in
3.8 cm

SCAT WIDTH

Similar species: Broad trail of five-toed, clawed track with a tail drag separates the snapping turtle tracks and trail.

Other sign: Nest in open area where sun warms sand and eggs. Nest may be several inches deep.

front
1.6 x 2.0 in
4.0 x 5.0 cm

hind
3.2 x 2.6 in
8.0 x 6.4 cm

FRONT TRACK LENGTH

FRONT TRACK WIDTH

Atlantic Loggerhead Turtle
Caretta caretta

A very large sea
turtle, weighing
170 to 350 pounds
(80 to 160 kg). Reddish-
brown color with five or
more coastal (side) plates.

Track: Flipper-shaped limbs with
two claws leave two holes in the sand.
In hard sand, only the front end of the
flipper may show. Footprints may be
obliterated by the dragging motion of
front legs scraping the sand. Hind feet
often only a drag mark.

Trail: Walking stride about 12.0
inches (30.0 cm). Straddle is wide
compared to stride, 28.0 to 36.0
inches (70.0 to 90.0 cm). Front feet,
which sweep backward and in, regis-
ter well outside the shell drag mark which is 8.0 to 12.0 inches
(20.0 to 30.0 cm) wide. Front feet may push up mounds of sand.
Hind feet often show only as drag marks.

Scat: Not known; turtle defecates in water.

Habitat: Ocean beaches.

sand mound with flipper kick marks

Similar species: Broad dragging trail of shell with parallel rows of two holes on each side of shell drag mark separates sea turtles from other turtles.

Other sign: Nests 12.0 inches (30.0 cm) deep are dug in beach sand.

front
6.0 to 10.0 x 3.0 to 6.0 in
15.0 to 25.0 x 7.5 to 15.0 cm

movement

front flipper marks

rear flipper marks

bottom of shell marks

hind
6.0 to 8.0 x 5.0 to 7.0 in
15.0 to 20.0 x 12.5 to 18.0 cm

FRONT TRACK LENGTH

FRONT TRACK WIDTH

Northern Fence Lizard
Sceloporus undulatus

Roughly the size of a roll of Life Savers; body about 3.0 inches (7.5 cm), with dry skin and ridged scales. Gray to dark brown above, with black crossbars or longitudinal stripes. Blue patches surrounded by black on side of throat. Considerable subspecies variation.

Track: Five relatively long, thin toes on front and hind feet. Hind heel is relatively long. Claws may show and be detached.

Trail: Trotting stride is about 3.0 inches (7.5 cm). Hind feet mostly register on top of front feet. Relatively wide straddle. Straight tail drag.

Scat: Brown cord, up to six to eight times longer than wide. White nitrogenous material usually found on one end.

Habitat: Wide variety of habitats including forests, woodland, and rock outcrops. Shelters in bushes, trees, under rocks, or in logs.

scat
1.5 x 0.25 in
3.8 x 0.6 cm

SCAT WIDTH

Similar species: Differs from salamanders by having five narrow toes on front feet and straighter tail drag. Differs from horned lizard by narrower footprint.

Other sign: Scuff marks in dust may indicate a dust bath.

detached claw

front
0.8 x 0.25 in
2.0 x 0.6 cm

hind
1.0 x 0.3 in
2.5 x 0.8 cm

slow walk

FRONT TRACK LENGTH

FRONT TRACK WIDTH

Snakes
various species

A variety of snakes, from garter snakes (*Thamnophis sirtalis*) to milk snakes (*Lampropeltis triangulum*) to rattlesnakes (*Crotalus horridus*).

Rattlesnake
Crotalus horridus

Track: No footprint to describe.

Trail: Varies from 1.0 to 4.0 inches (2.5 to 10.0 cm) wide. Characterized by side-to-side undulations of the trail. The period, the distance from one curve to the next, varies by species, age, and speed of the snake. Surface material is usually pushed up at the outside of each curve. Gait is either a side-to-side undulation or sidewinding.

Scat: Black or brown cord, with constrictions and undulations. White nitrogenous material often attached.

Habitat: Varies widely, from water's edge to rock outcrops to dry sand dunes.

scat
4.0 x 0.4 in
20.0 x 1.0 cm

shed skin

SCAT WIDTH

Similar species: Resembles no other track.

Other sign: Shed skin.

lateral undulatory

sidewinding

trail

Common Loon
Gavia immer

Large-size, long-bodied aquatic bird, average length 24.0 inches (60.0 cm). Dark-colored bird with black-and-white-checkered back and neck band. Dark-greenish head.

Track: Three toes showing, toes 2 to 4 pointing forward. Toe 1 does not register. Toes 2, 3, and 4 have claws and distal webbing.

Trail: Walking stride is 10.0 inches (25.0 cm) with a 7.0-inch (18.0-cm) straddle. Toes turn inward. Foot drag marks usually evident because the loon's legs are placed far back on its body making walking difficult and causing the loon to drag its feet.

nest

Scat: Not known.

Habitat: Freshwater lakes and rivers; near shore on ocean.

Similar species: Differs from all other aquatic birds by heavy drag marks in trail and relatively long, narrow feet.

Other sign: Large nest on reeds and brush at edge of water. Eggs appear large in small nest.

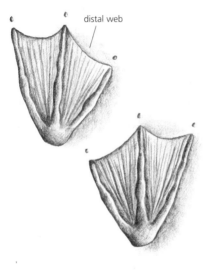

distal web

feet
5.25 x 4.3 in
13.1 x 10.8 cm

walk

TRACK LENGTH

TRACK WIDTH (50%)

White Pelican
Pelecanus erythrorhynchos

Large aquatic bird, average length more
than 60.0 inches (150.0 cm),
with a wingspan of
more than 8.0 feet
(2.4 m). White
with black
primary wing
feathers. Large
bill is yellow to
orange.

Track: Four long, slender toes. Toe 1
offset to side of track. Feet *totipalmate,*
with webbing between all four toes.
Webbing distal and slightly convex
between toes. Claws attached.

Trail: Walking stride averages 16.0
inches (40.0 cm). Toes turn inward.

Scat: Shapeless, brownish-white mass.

Habitat: Lakes, marshes, and bays. During summer, found in
freshwater lakes; in winter, found in saltwater.

ground nest

Similar species: Differs from all other web-footed birds except cormorant by being toti-palmate. Differs from cormorant by having attached claws.

Other sign: Nests on ground in large island colonies.

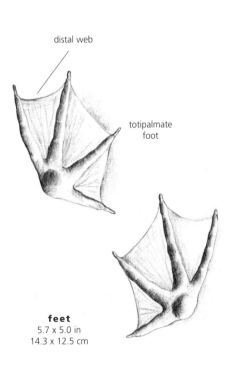

distal web

totipalmate foot

feet
5.7 x 5.0 in
14.3 x 12.5 cm

walk

TRACK LENGTH

TRACK WIDTH (50%)

Double-crested Cormorant
Phalacrocorax auritus

Large aquatic bird, average length more than 32.0 inches (80.0 cm), with a wingspan of more than 4.3 feet (132.0 cm). Dark-colored body with orange throat patch. Crest of two white feathers behind eye, which may be difficult to see.

Track: Four long, slender toes. Toe 1 offset to side of track. Toe 4 is longest. Feet *totipalmate,* i.e., with webbing between all four toes. Webbing distal and slightly convex between toes. Claws detached.

Trail: Walking stride is about 10.0 inches (25.0 cm). Walks awkwardly on land, with a short stride for its size. Toes turn inward.

nest

Scat: Shapeless, nearly liquid white mass.

Habitat: Saltwater islands, bays, and cliffs. Freshwater lakes, ponds, and swamps.

Similar species: Differs from all other web-footed birds except pelican by being totipalmate. Differs from pelican by having detached claws.

Other sign: Nests in colonies on ground or in trees. Acidic scat kills trees and ground vegetation.

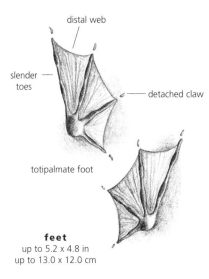

distal web

slender toes

detached claw

totipalmate foot

feet
up to 5.2 x 4.8 in
up to 13.0 x 12.0 cm

walk

TRACK LENGTH

TRACK WIDTH (50%)

Green Heron
Butorides virescens (striatus)

Medium-size wading bird, average length 14.0 inches (36.0 cm). Male and female similar in overall appearance: blue to greenish body, with reddish-brown neck and yellowish legs.

Track: Four toes, toes 2 to 4 pointing forward. Small proximal web between toes 3 and 4. Footprint is asymmetrical, with toe 1 set to inside of foot axis (drawn through toe 3). On hard ground, metatarsal pad may not show (that is, toes may appear unconnected).

← 12.0 in →

nest
4 to 5 eggs common

cough pellet

Trail: Walking stride about 10.0 inches (25.0 cm). Trail is fairly straight and feet point forward.

Scat: Semiliquid, predominantly white. Solid cords of scat vary from 1.0 to 2.0 inches (2.5 to 5.0 cm) and may contain fish, insects, frogs, and salamanders.

Habitat: Fresh- and saltwater areas along ponds, streams, lakes, swamps, and beaches where heavily wooded.

Similar species: Smaller version of great blue heron track (6.5 in/16.5 cm). Differs from other shore-edge tracks by asymmetrical placement of toes.

Other sign: Undigested material may be coughed up as pellets.

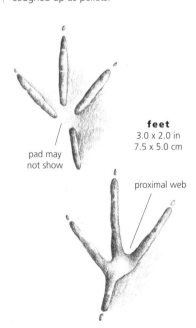

pad may not show

feet
3.0 x 2.0 in
7.5 x 5.0 cm

proximal web

walk

TRACK LENGTH

TRACK WIDTH

Great Blue Heron
Ardea herodias

**Large wading bird, average
length 45.0 inches (113.0 cm).
Male and female similar in overall appearance: gray-blue body,
with white neck and yellow beak.
Black crown extends on feathers off
rear of head.**

Track: Four toes, toes 2 to 4 pointing forward. Small proximal web
between toes 3 and 4. Footprint is asymmetrical, with toe 1 set to inside of foot
axis (drawn through toe 3). Toe 1 is
about 1.5 inches (3.8 cm); toe 2 is longer
than 1, though shorter than 3 and 4. On
hard ground, metatarsal pad may not
show (that is, toes may appear unconnected).

Trail: Walking stride about 20.0 inches
(50.0 cm). Trail is fairly straight and feet
point forward.

cough pellet

nest

rookery

Scat: Semiliquid, predominantly white. Solid cords of scat vary from 2.0 to 3.0 inches (5.0 to 7.5 cm) in length, and may contain fish, frogs, salamanders, and even small rodents. Ground beneath nests becomes coated with droppings.

Habitat: Frequents backwater eddies along riverbanks, shallow edges of lakes, and tide-flats.

Similar species: Differs from other shore-edge tracks by large size and asymmetrical placement of toes.

Other sign: Large colonies of nests high in trees. Undigested material may be coughed up as pellets.

pad may not show

feet
6.5 x 5.25 in
16.0 x 13.1 cm

proximal web

offset toes

walk

Mute Swan
Cygnus olor

Large aquatic bird, length averaging 60.0 inches (150.0 cm). Male larger than female. Adult is all white, with an orange bill with a black knob at base. Immature swan has gray plumage. Male and female identically colored. Swims with curved neck and arched wings.

Track: Four toes. Toes 2 to 4, which point forward, usually register. Toe 1 points rearward and only occasionally shows. Distal webbing between toes 2, 3, and 4. Toes 2 and 4 tend to converge slightly near tips. Claws are broad, blunt, and attached to toes. Feet turned in.

rare

rare

Trail: Walking stride is about 14.0 inches (35.0 cm).

Scat: Cord, five to eight times longer than wide. Often greenish and coated with white nitrogenous deposits.

scat
3.5 x 0.5 in
8.8 x 1.3 cm

SCAT WIDTH

Habitat: Ponds, lakes, swamps, and slowly flowing streams and rivers, all with emergent vegetation.

Similar species: Larger than ducks and geese. Differs from pelican and cormorant by lacking webbing between toes 1 and 2. Larger than gulls, also differing from them by having convergent toes and distal webbing.

Other sign: Nests on elevated areas such as cattails, reeds, or roots. Eggs larger than eggs of Canada goose.

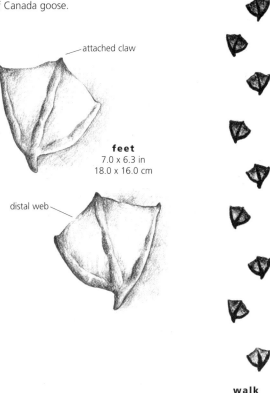

attached claw

feet
7.0 x 6.3 in
18.0 x 16.0 cm

distal web

walk

TRACK LENGTH (50%)

TRACK WIDTH (50%)

Sandhill Crane
Grus canadensis

Large bird, average length 39.0 inches (98.0 cm). Appearance of males and females similar: grayish, with red crown on head, and white cheeks and chin.

Track: Four toes, toes 2 to 4 showing. Outside toes opposed by nearly 180 degrees. Toe 3 is longer than 2 and 4. Small proximal web between toes 2 and 3 rarely shows. Claws usually attached to toes, though claw of toe 1 rarely shows. Feet point forward.

Trail: Walking stride about 24.0 inches (60.0 cm). Often runs, extending its stride. Tracks have a narrow straddle, being nearly in line with one another.

Scat: Similar to, but smaller than, Canada goose. Brown in color, with some vegetation. Can contain bones of small mammals, reptiles, and amphibians.

Habitat: Meadows, marshes, grasslands, and fields.

scat
2.5 x 0.3 in
6.3 x .8 cm

SCAT WIDTH

Similar species: Differs from ducks, geese, swans, and herons by having only small proximal web (if it shows). Differs from large raptors by lacking toe 1.

Other sign: Listen for its rattling call, which suggests to some a sound that dinosaurs may have made.

attached claw

detached claw

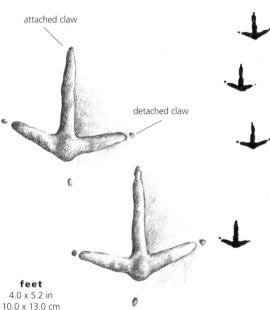

feet
4.0 x 5.2 in
10.0 x 13.0 cm

walk

TRACK LENGTH

TRACK WIDTH (50%)

Ducks
various species

Mallard
Anas platyrhynchos

Aquatic birds with webbed feet, varying in size from the small bufflehead (*Bucephala albeola*) through mallards to pintails (*Anas acuta*). Length ranges from 14.0 to 24.0 inches (35.0 to 60.0 cm). Large variety in body patterns among species. Males generally more brightly colored than females.

Track: Four toes. Toes 2 to 4, which point forward, usually register. Toe 1 points rearward and may not show. Distal webbing between toes 2, 3, and 4. Webbing concave between toes. Toes 2 and 4 tend to converge near tips. Claws are broad, blunt, and attached to toes. Feet turned in.

Trail: Walking stride of a mallard (illustrated here) is about 4.0 inches (10.0 cm).

scat
2.0 x 0.25 in
5.0 x 0.8 cm

SCAT WIDTH

Scat: Pencil-size cords, four to eight times longer than wide. Often greenish and coated with white nitrogenous deposits.

Habitat: Ponds, lakes, marshes, streams, rivers, and bays.

Similar species: Tracks differ from geese and swan tracks by smaller size. Differ from pelicans and cormorants by lacking webbing between toes 1 and 2. Differ from gulls by having convergent toes.

Other sign: Nests may be on the ground, in tree cavities, or on floating mats. Eggs roughly the size of chicken eggs, though there may be great variation among species.

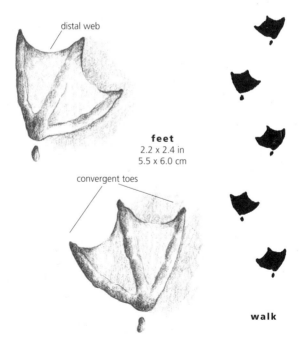

distal web

feet
2.2 x 2.4 in
5.5 x 6.0 cm

convergent toes

walk

TRACK LENGTH

TRACK WIDTH

Canada Goose
Branta canadensis

Medium-size aquatic bird, average length 30.0 inches (75.0 cm). Considerable size variation among sub-species. Black head and neck, with a white chin band. Back is olive brown. Male and female similarly colored.

Track: Four toes. Toes 2 to 4, which point forward, usually register. Toe 1 points rearward and only occasionally shows. Distal webbing between toes 2, 3, and 4. Toes 2 and 4 tend to converge slightly near tips. Claws are broad, blunt, and usually attached to toes. Feet turn in.

Trail: Walking stride is about 12.0 inches (30.0 cm).

scat
3.0 x 0.4 in
7.5 x 1.0 cm

SCAT WIDTH

Scat: Cord, five to eight times longer than wide. Often greenish and coated with white nitrogenous deposits. As long as 3.5 inches (8.8 cm).

Habitat: Ponds, lakes, marshes, streams, rivers, and bays.

Similar species: Larger than most ducks and smaller than swans. Differs from pelican and cormorant by lacking webbing between toes 1 and 2. Larger than gulls, and differing from them by having convergent toes and distal webbing.

Other sign: Nests on ground, sometimes on cliff ledges, and in abandoned heron and raptor nests. Eggs larger than chicken eggs.

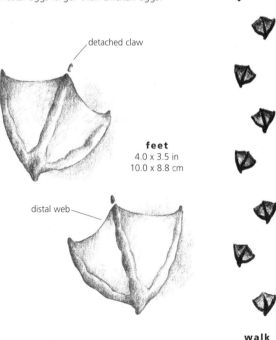

detached claw

feet
4.0 x 3.5 in
10.0 x 8.8 cm

distal web

walk

TRACK LENGTH

TRACK WIDTH

Hawks
various species

Medium-size birds, up to 25.0 inches (63.0 cm) in length, with wingspans of 50.0 inches (125.0 cm). The red-tailed hawk (*Buteo jamaicensis*) shown here is a highly variable, dark-colored hawk with red tail feathers. Light phase has a dark belly band.

Track: Four wide, robust toes. Toes 2 to 4 point forward. Claws are long, sharp, and not attached to the toe print.

Trail: Walking stride of a red-tailed hawk (illustrated here) is about 12.0 inches (30.0 cm). Hops or runs after prey on the ground. Claws may drag in soft mud, creating a fringe along sides of footprint.

Scat: Semiliquid, primarily white with some brown intermixed. Unlike owls, scat is ejected with force, sometimes leaving a trail. Whitish piles and vertical streaks below nests.

cough pellets

Habitat: Woodland and open country with scattered trees.

Similar species: Smaller than eagles. Differ from owls by having three toes pointing forward. Differ from geese and swans by lacking webbing. Differ from herons and cranes by having symmetrical feet.

Other sign: Cough pellets may be 1.5 to 4.0 inches (3.8 to 10.0 cm) long.

walk

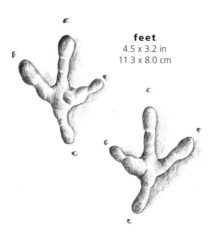

feet
4.5 x 3.2 in
11.3 x 8.0 cm

TRACK LENGTH

TRACK WIDTH

Eagles
two species

Large birds, averaging
35.0 inches (90.0 cm) in
length, with wingspans
of 80.0 inches (200.0
cm). Brown bodies.
Adult golden eagle
(*Aquila chrysaetos*) has
golden feathers over head and
neck. Adult bald eagle (*Haliaeetus leucocephalus*) has white head, neck, and tail feathers.

Bald eagle
Haliaeetus leucocephalus

Track: Four wide, robust toes. Toes 2 to 4 point forward. Lacks webbing and metatarsal pad. Claws are long, sharp, and not attached to the toe print.

Trail: Walking stride about 18.0 inches (45.0 cm). Golden eagle will run after prey on the ground.

Scat: Semiliquid, primarily white with some brown intermixed.

Habitat: Golden eagle found in hilly areas and hunts over open country. Bald eagle usually found near lakes and rivers.

cough pellet

urine stain on rock

Similar species: Larger than hawk's track, which is less than 3.0 inches (7.5 cm). Differs from owls by having three toes pointing forward. Differs from geese and swans by lacking webbing. Differs from herons and cranes by having symmetrical feet.

Other sign: Cough pellets may be 5.0 x 1.5 inches (12.5 x 3.8 cm). Nests may be 6.0 feet (2.0 m) in diameter.

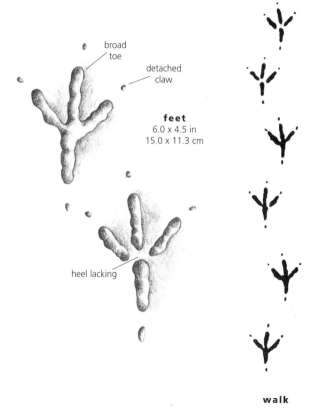

broad toe

detached claw

feet
6.0 x 4.5 in
15.0 x 11.3 cm

heel lacking

walk

Ruffed Grouse
Bonasa umbellus

Size comparable to a chicken, 17.0
inches (43.0 cm) in length.
Mottled brown in color.
Black feather ruffs on
side of neck. Wide,
multibanded tail with
dark band near tip.

Track: Four toes, with toes 2 to 4 pointing forward. Toe 1, relatively short, may
not show. Toes are relatively wide and
lack webbing. Claws detached. In winter,
a fringe of scales makes toes wider.
Metatarsal present and may be attached
to toes.

Trail: Walking stride is about 9.0 inches
(23.0 cm). Trail is straight and feet toe in.
In deep snow, there can be a trough, 4.0
inches (10.0 cm) wide. Look for wing marks in the snow as well
as body impression under brush and evergreen trees.

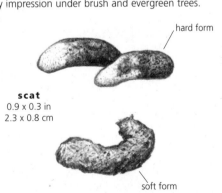

hard form

scat
0.9 x 0.3 in
2.3 x 0.8 cm

soft form

Scat: Light to dark brown, sometimes with white nitrogenous covering. Content includes buds, berries, and sawdust. In winter, deposited in snow nest in large mass of fifty or so scats. May be scattered if roosting in trees.

Habitat: Mixed deciduous woodlands with dense understory. Prefers aspen groves.

Similar species: Tracks larger than bobwhite. Differ from other forest birds by wide, robust toe size and short toe 1. Grouse trails can be differentiated from those of other forest birds by their short stride.

Other sign: Burrow under the snow to roost. Round nests made from leaves, usually 5.0 inches (13.0 cm) in diameter, and brush. Dust baths in sandy areas.

walk

detached claw

feet
2.0 x 1.4 in
5.0 x 3.6 cm

TRACK LENGTH

TRACK WIDTH

Turkey
Meleagris gallopavo

Large, ground-dwelling bird. Males average 45.0 inches (113.0 cm) and females 35.0 inches (88.0 cm) in length. Smaller and more slender than the domesticated Thanksgiving turkey. Male has a dark-brown to black body, with white stripes on flight feather; tail feathers are tipped with brownish white. Color of female's feathers is similar but dull. Male also has red *wattles*, folds of skin hanging from the chin.

Track: Four broad, robust toes. Toes 2 to 4 face forward. Hind toe (toe 1) only occasionally registers, and then in a straight line with toe 4. Only the claw or tip of toe 1 registers. Metatarsal pad present, though it may be unattached to toes. Claws narrow and usually attached to toe.

Trail: Walking stride 15.0 inches (38.0 cm). Foot axis may vary, pointing into the line of travel or turning slightly out.

scat
3.0 x 0.5 in
7.5 x 1.3 cm

tracks with scratch marks

SCAT WIDTH

Scat: Solid scat is long, up to 3.0 inches (7.5 cm), narrow, and brown with greenish-white nitrogenous material on ends. Also produces a soft scat that piles in a shapeless mass on ground.

Habitat: Open forest, shrubland, and wooded swamps, in trees with lateral branches for roosting at night.

Similar species: Differs from other birds by wide, robust toes. Tracks larger than other ground-dwelling birds. Lacks webbing of ducks and certain other aquatic birds. Separated from eagles by presence (usually) of metatarsal pad. Toes 2 and 4 point forward to a greater degree than those of crane.

Other sign: Scratches on ground where turkey digs for seeds, acorns, nuts, and insects.

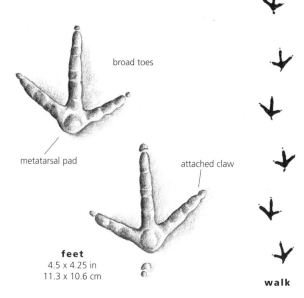

broad toes

metatarsal pad

attached claw

feet
4.5 x 4.25 in
11.3 x 10.6 cm

walk

TRACK LENGTH

TRACK WIDTH (50%)

Bobwhite
Colinus virginianus

Size comparable to a small chicken, 9.0 inches (23.0 cm) in length. Mottled reddish-brown with a short gray-colored tail. Male with white stripes on face and throat, brownish in female.

Track: Four toes, with toes 2 to 4 pointing forward. Toe 1, relatively short, may be detached or not show. Toes are relatively wide and lack webbing. Feet point forward to slightly inward. Metatarsal present.

Trail: Walking stride is about 6.0 inches (15.0 cm). Trail is straight but feet toe in.

Scat: Light to dark brown, sometimes with white nitrogenous covering.

depressions in dust from chicks

scat
1.4 x 0.2 in
3.5 x 0.5 cm

Habitat: Tall grasslands, brush lands, open woodlands, and cultivated fields.

Similar species: Tracks smaller than grouse. Differ from other forest birds by wide, robust toe size and short toe 1. Bobwhite trails can be differentiated from those of other forest birds by their short strides and wide straddles.

Other sign: Ground roost is a circle of shallow body depressions where birds sleep with their heads pointing out. Nest is a shallow depression under "woven" grass with a side entrance.

walk

feet
1.75 x 1.5 in
4.4 x 3.8 cm

TRACK LENGTH

TRACK WIDTH

Ring-necked Pheasant
Phasianus colchicus

A large chicken-like bird, males 33.0 inches (84.0 cm) and females 21.0 inches (53.0 cm) in length. Male brightly colored with green head, mottled brown, black, bronze, and white body. Female is a mottled buffy brown. Male has a long, pointed tail.

Track: Four toes, with toes 2 to 4 pointing forward. Toe 1, relatively short, may not show. Toes are relatively wide and lack webbing. Feet point forward to slightly inward. Metatarsal pad may show and may be unattached to toes.

Trail: Walking stride is about 11.0 inches (28.0 cm). Narrow trail; toes neither toe in or toe out.

scat
0.8 x 0.4 in
2.0 x 1.0 cm

SCAT WIDTH

Scat: Variable bulbous dropping, greenish-brown with white ends. Sometimes two or more pieces sticking together.

Habitat: Bushy country, woodland edges, farmlands, and wind rows.

Similar species: Differ from grouse by longer stride and narrower straddle. Smaller tracks differentiate from turkey.

Other sign: Nest in grass is a shallow depression occasionally lined with some grass.

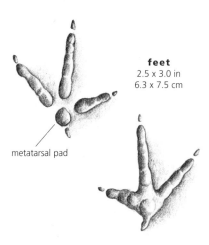

feet
2.5 x 3.0 in
6.3 x 7.5 cm

metatarsal pad

walk

Coot
Fulica americana

Medium-size aquatic bird, average length 15.0 inches (38.0 cm). Slate-black body, with white beak extending into small brown forehead shield.

Track: Four toes showing, toes 2 to 4 pointing forward. Toe 1 angles inward. Toes 2, 3, and 4 have fringe of webbing with indented lobes. Long, pointed claws, especially those on toe 1, may be separated from toes.

Trail: Walking stride 10.0 inches (25.0 cm); tends to wander when walking. Foot axis parallel to line of travel.

Scat: White liquid.

Habitat: Freshwater lakes and ponds having shallow water where reeds and rushes grow.

Similar species: Differs from all other aquatic birds by the indented lobes on each toe.

Other sign: Floating nest built from cattails, sedges, and rushes, rising several inches above the water.

indented lobe

feet
5.2 x 4.8 in
13.0 x 12.0 cm

walk

TRACK LENGTH

TRACK WIDTH (50%)

Shorebirds
various species

Avocet
Recurvirostra americana

Many birds, such as avocet, sandpipers, killdeer, curlews, and snipes. Length varies from 6.0 to 18.0 inches (15.0 to 45.0 cm). All have similar footprints and differentiation is difficult.

Track: Four narrow toes, although toe 1 may not show. Toes 2 to 4 face forward and are nearly symmetrical around toe 3. Outer toe angle often greater than 120 degrees. Small, proximal webbing between toes 2, 3, and 4 may be visible, though curlews and sandpipers have proximal webbing only between toes 3 and 4. Metatarsal pad may show; avocets (illustrated here) with mesial webbing.

Trail: Shorebirds are constantly running along the water's edge. Stride varies from 4.0 to 20.0 inches (10.0 to 50.0 cm).

Scat: Small and semiliquid. Brown, green, and white mixed.

Habitat: Water's edge at lakes, rivers, streams, bays, and wastewater treatment plants.

nest in grass with twigs

Similar species: Differ from songbirds or perching birds by the weak showing of toe 1, which in perching birds is strong and used to grasp branches. Outer toe angle of songbirds is less than 90 degrees. Shorebirds walk or run, but most songbirds hop.

Other sign: Myriad roundish holes where beak pushed into the sand in pursuit of insects.

feet
2.4 x 2.9 in
6.0 x 7.3 cm

may not show

walk

TRACK LENGTH

TRACK WIDTH

Gulls
various species

Average length 25.0 inches (63.0 cm). Pale-gray back, white head. Tips of primary feathers black. Yellow bill with red spot; pink legs. Herring gull (*Larus argentatus*) illustrated here. Many species, such as Bonaparte's, Franklin's, Ring-billed, and Herring gulls. Length varies from 11.0 to 30.0 inches. Gregarious species of open beaches of lakes, oceans, and rivers.

Herring gull
Larus argentatus

Track: Four toes. Toes 2 to 4 (forward-pointing) show. Toe 1 may register only slightly or not show at all. Webbing relatively straight between toes. Toes 2 and 3 tend to diverge, especially at the tips.

Trail: Walking stride of herring gull is about 13.0 inches (33.0 cm). Feet turn slightly inward.

Scat: Semiliquid. Primarily white, with indistinguishable contents.

cough pellet

Habitat: Along coast and on inland lakes and rivers. Nest in colonies on ground or cliffs, usually on islands. Nest is made of grass or seaweed. A scavenger, the herring gull is also found at dumps.

Similar species: Differ from ducks, swans, and geese by having divergent toes. Smaller than swans and geese. Differ from coot by having webbing between toes.

Other sign: Cough pellets containing bones, fish scales, urchin parts, and garbage. Shell fragments from dropping mussel shells onto rocks from high in the air.

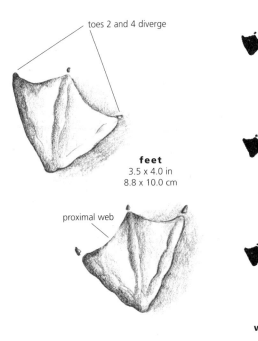

toes 2 and 4 diverge

feet
3.5 x 4.0 in
8.8 x 10.0 cm

proximal web

walk

TRACK LENGTH

TRACK WIDTH (50%)

Owls
various species

Considerable variation in length, from the saw-whet owl (*Aegolius acadicus*), 8.0 inches (20.0 cm), to the short-eared owl (*Asio flammeus*) illustrated here, 15.0 inches (38.0 cm), to the great horned owl (*Bubo virginianus*), 25.0 inches (63.0 cm). All species have immobile eyes offset by facial disks of feathers. Great variability in appearance among species. Typical body colors are grays, browns, and reddish browns.

Short-eared owl
Asio flammeus

Track: Four broad toes, with two paired and facing forward. Toe 4 position is not fixed and may face back or out. Lack webbing and metatarsal pads. Claws long and detached from footprint. Tracks of short-eared owl illustrated here.

Trail: Walking stride varies considerably among species, from 3.0 to 10.0 inches (7.5 to 25.0 cm).

cough pellet

perch branch

cough pellets

perch with pellets

Scat: Semiliquid, primarily white.

Habitat: Forested areas. Some species, such as barn owls, will readily use human structures.

Similar species: Differ from most birds in toes 2 and 3 being paired, nearly parallel, and pointing forward. Differ from woodpeckers by toes being wide and robust, and by toes 1 and 4 being much shorter than toes 2 and 3.

Other sign: Cough pellets below a roost. Diameter of cough pellets ranges from 0.25 to 1.0 inch (0.6 to 2.5 cm) and is directly related to the size of the owl. Pellets are shiny and black when new but turn gray with age.

detached
claw

feet
2.5 x 2.0 in
6.3 x 5.0 cm

walk

TRACK LENGTH

TRACK WIDTH

Woodpeckers
various species

Considerable variation in size. The flicker (*Colaptes auratus*), illustrated here, is a medium-size woodpecker, slightly larger than the American robin, average length 12.0 inches (30.0 cm). Male has brown-barred back, black chest, white rump, and red or black whisker stripe, and is yellow under wings. Female lacks whisker stripe.

Flicker
Colaptes auratus

Track: Four toes, with two parallel and pointing forward. Toes 1 and 4 point backward and are not equal in length. Strong, rigid tail feathers may show on ground.

Scat: Cord, about four or more times longer than wide. Often contains undigested parts of insects.

Habitat: Open woodlands, dense forests, and around towns.

Similar species: Differs from three-toed woodpecker by presence of toe 1. Differs from other birds its size by having two toes pointing forward.

Other sign: Excavates and nests in tree cavities. Does not add bedding material to cavity nest.

scat
1.0 x 0.25 in
2.5 x 0.6 cm

SCAT WIDTH

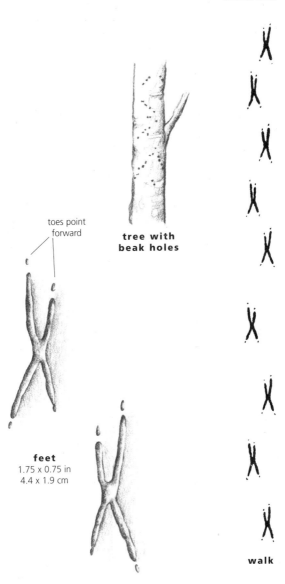

toes point forward

tree with beak holes

feet
1.75 x 0.75 in
4.4 x 1.9 cm

walk

TRACK LENGTH

TRACK WIDTH

Blue Jay
Cyanocitta cristata

**Small bird with
blue body and
white markings
on wings.
Prominent blue crest
and black throat band.
Average length about 11.0
inches (28.0 cm).**

Track: Narrow track with four narrow toes, toes 2 to 4 facing forward and not widely splayed. Toe 1 as long as toes 2, 3, and 4. Toe 1 broader than other toes. Lacks webbing and metatarsal pad. Claws long, especially on toe 1.

Trail: Hopping stride is 4.0 to 5.0 inches (10.0 to 12.5 cm). Occasionally walks.

Scat: Semiliquid, brown to black with white intermixed.

Habitat: Woodlands, gardens, and parks.

Similar species: Differs from songbirds by larger size and relatively narrow footprint. Smaller and narrower than crows and ravens.

Other sign: Nest, on horizontal branch or tree crotch, is compact and occasionally cemented with mud.

hop

feet
2.2 x 0.5 in
5.5 x 1.3 cm

heel lacking

walk

TRACK LENGTH

TRACK WIDTH

Crow
Corvus brachyrhynchos

Medium-size black bird (17.0 in / 43.0 cm) with strong beak (smaller than raven's). Sides of tail are parallel in flight, not wedge-shaped. Black feet and legs.

Track: Four toes, three facing forward. Toe 1 nearly equals toes 2, 3, and 4. Lacks webbing. Metatarsal pad present. Claws long and often detached from footprint. The footprint length of 2.5 inches (6.3 cm) includes toe 4, which adds 0.7 inches (1.8 cm).

Trail: Walking stride varies but is about 5.0 inches (13.0 cm). Crows both walk and hop and may run with a long stride.

Scat: Semiliquid brown and white, but may contain remnants of food from their omnivorous diet.

cough pellet

Habitat: Roadside, woodlands, farms, orchards, and lake and ocean shores.

Similar species: Raven track and trail is much larger than crow's. Lack the paired forward-facing toes of owls. Lack long toe 1 of hawks.

Other sign: Cough pellets up to 1.0 x 0.4 inches (2.5 x 1.0 cm). Pellets may contain berries, seeds, nuts, insect parts, and snails, among other items of its varied diet.

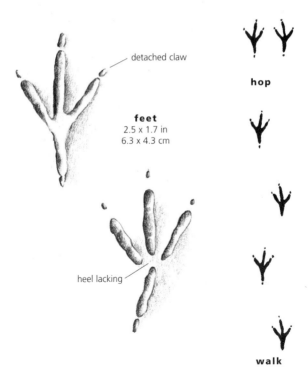

detached claw

feet
2.5 x 1.7 in
6.3 x 4.3 cm

heel lacking

hop

walk

TRACK LENGTH

TRACK WIDTH

Common Raven
Corvus corax

Large black bird, length averaging 24.0 inches (60.0 cm). Beak thick and robust. Tail is wedge-shaped in flight. Size varies considerably, though male is larger than female.

Track: Four toes, toes 2 to 4 facing forward. Length of toe 1 nearly equals toes 2, 3, and 4. Lacks webbing and metatarsal pad. Claws long and detached from footprint.

Trail: Walking stride varies considerably, but is about 20.0 inches (50.0 cm). Also runs, with a longer stride.

Scat: Semiliquid, brown, black, and white. Often oily. May contain remnants of its omnivorous diet.

Habitat: Tree areas, especially where carcasses of deer can be found, and at garbage dumps. Will beg food from picnickers.

cough pellet

Similar species: Track and trail of the common crow are diminutive versions of the raven's. Lacks the paired forward-facing toes of owls. Lacks the long toe 1 of hawks. Smaller than eagle's.

Other sign: Cough pellets up to 3.0 x 0.5 inches (7.5 x 1.3 cm). Caches food in forks of trees and, often, by burying.

detached claw

feet
3.8 x 2.0 in
9.5 x 5.0 cm

heel
lacking

hop

walk

TRACK LENGTH

TRACK WIDTH

Opossum
Didelphis viginiana (marsupialis)

The size of a large
domestic cat, but
more stout,
nearly hairless,
and with a round, rat-
like tail. Weight varies
from 8.0 to 14.0 pounds (3.5
to 6.5 kg). Face whitish, with thin,
black-edged ears. Body is whitish with
gray and black hairs interspersed.

Track: Five toes. Hind print is distinctive, with an opposable (like the human thumb) inside toe protruding sideways from other toes and lacking a claw. Outside toe is slightly separated from middle three toes. Front footprint is wider than long and shows long toes that widen slightly toward the end.

Trail: Walking stride 18.0 inches (45.0 cm). Walking trail often reflects slow movement, with hind footprint registering behind the front. Trail is sloppy and footprints seldom register directly. Tail drag often shows. Walking pattern occasionally similar to that of the raccoon, where the hind footprint registers beside the front footprint.

scat shape is highly variable

scat
4.0 x 0.5 in
10.0 x 1.3 cm

SCAT WIDTH

Scat: Highly variable shape and size and lack of distinctive form reflect highly variable, omnivorous diet. Single scat may be up to 4.0 inches (10.0 cm) long.

Habitat: Prefers riparian areas, woodlands, and farmyards. Habitat is not restricted by diet, as the opossum will eat small mammals, birds, eggs, reptiles, amphibians, fish, carrion, fruit, and any garbage it can find.

Similar species: Trail may be confused with those of muskrats, woodrats, and domestic rats when a tail drag is present. However, the distinctive hind footprint and large size of the opossum footprint identify its trail.

Other sign: Dens in logs, stumps, rock crevices, and dens of other animals.

walk

front
1.5 x 2.1 in
3.8 x 5.3 cm

hind
2.2 x 1.9 in
5.5 x 4.8 cm

opposable toe

slow walk

FRONT TRACK LENGTH

FRONT TRACK WIDTH

Shrews
various species

Masked shrew
Sorex cinereus

Smaller than mice, less than 0.25 ounce (7.0 g). Long, pointed nose. Minute eyes and ears. Color brown to black, with gray to white belly. Eat mostly insects. The masked shrew (*Sorex cinereus*) is illustrated here.

Track: Five slender toes are present on front and hind feet. In clear prints, four interdigital and two proximal pads may be seen.

Trail: Hopping stride seldom more than 2.0 inches (5.0 cm). The group of tracks is less than 1.0 inches (2.5 cm) long. Seldom is the stride more than three times the group.

Scat: Usually small pellets with tapered ends.

Habitat: Found everywhere from grasslands to rolling hills. Look for tracks in wet, fine mud of riparian areas or in snow along logs

—— tapered ends

scat
0.2 x 0.1 in
0.5 x 0.3 cm

SCAT WIDTH

insect remains

or the edges of buildings. Wood piles and leaf litter make good homes.

Similar species: Differ from mice and voles by having five toes on front foot.

Other sign: After eating, leave body parts from insects they have killed. Often burrow just below the surface of the snow, opening tunnels that partially collapse and expose their route. Trails in the snow radiate from holes like spokes of a wheel.

front
0.25 x 0.2 in
0.6 x 0.5 cm

two proximal pads

detached
interdigital pad

six pads

furred heel, not included
in track measurement

hind
0.3 x 0.2 in
0.8 x 0.5 cm

bound

FRONT TRACK LENGTH

FRONT TRACK WIDTH

Red Fox
Vulpes vulpes

Jack Russell
terrier–size,
6.0 to 15.0
pounds (3.0 to
7.0 kg).
Reddish yellow,
with black stockings
and a white tip on the
tail. Color phases include silver, black, cross, and bluish gray.
Long, pointed ears and elongate, pointed muzzle.

Track: Claws prominent. One lobe on the leading edge of the interdigital pad. Inside toe slightly larger than outside. A ridge of callus present across interdigital pad, but difficult to detect on hind footprint. Front foot larger than hind.

Trail: Trotting stride averages 32.0 inches (80.0 cm). Typically uses a trotting gait and, occasionally, a 2 x 2 trot with body turned to the side. Walks more than coyote, especially in shrubs.

Scat: Often has tapered tail. Composition varies. Mouse or rabbit fur, berries, and insects are common. Bird feathers and plant remains often present.

scat
2.0 x 0.6 in
5.0 x 1.5 cm

log

SCAT WIDTH

Habitat: Found in a variety of habitats from brush to croplands to mixed hard- and softwood forest. Prefers edges, where hunting for small mammals is good. Also found in urban areas, where cover is available during the daytime. Not found in dense forests.

Similar species: Differs from other canids by having a ridge of callus on the interdigital pad. Track tends to be larger than gray fox, and usually shows claws. Differs from bobcat in having only one lobe on the interdigital pad and claws (usually) showing.

Other sign: Multiple dens are used each season. Often digs own den. A given den may be used for several years. Look for small bones around den entrance. Scat has a diagnostic musky odor, produced by a musk gland on the top of the tail. Learn to identify this unique foxy odor. Foxes tightrope-walk on narrow logs. May take over woodchuck dens.

side trot

trot

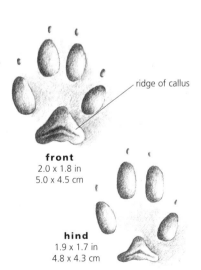

ridge of callus

front
2.0 x 1.8 in
5.0 x 4.5 cm

hind
1.9 x 1.7 in
4.8 x 4.3 cm

FRONT TRACK LENGTH

FRONT TRACK WIDTH

Gray Fox
Urocyon cinereoargenteus

Larger than
a miniature
poodle, 8.0 to
11.0 pounds
(4.0 to 5.0 kg).
Body color is
pepper-and-salt.
A black stripe
runs down the
back and upper
side of tail. Sides are reddish. Tip of tail is black. Long,
pointed ears and elongate, pointed muzzle.

Track: Small for a canid, somewhat broad and therefore somewhat catlike. Claws, rarely present in track, are very small and sharp, giving the gray fox the ability to climb trees like a cat. Front foot larger than hind.

Trail: Generally a trot. Trotting stride averages 24.0 inches (60.0 cm). Walks more than coyote.

Scat: Often has tapered tail. Composition varies, as the gray fox is opportunistic when feeding. Rabbit fur is most common, followed by fur of other small mammals, berries, and insects. Plant remains are often present.

scat
2.0 x 0.6 in
5.0 x 1.5 cm

Habitat: Prefers a mixture of fields and early stage woodlands. More often found in woodlands than is red fox.

Similar species: Smaller than coyote and wolf. Lacks the ridge of callus on the interdigital pad of the red fox. Differs from coyote in that claws often do not show.

Other sign: Seldom digs dens, but makes use of woodpiles, rock outcrops, hollow trees, and brushpiles. Look for small bones around den entrances.

side trot

climbing tree

front
1.8 x 1.6 in
4.5 x 4.0 cm

no callus ridge

hind
1.7 x 1.6 in
4.3 x 4.0 cm

trot

FRONT TRACK LENGTH

FRONT TRACK WIDTH

Coyote
Canis latrans

Smaller than a bor-
der collie, 20.0 to
25.0 pounds (9.0 to
11.0 kg). Male larger
than female. Color varies
from completely gray to tan to
rust. Long, pointed ears and
long, narrow muzzle.

Track: Claws usually present. One lobe on the leading edge of the interdigital pad. Inside toe slightly larger than outside. Front foot larger than hind.

Trail: Trotting stride averages 41.0 inches (94.0 cm). Often uses a trot with body turned to the side, leaving a 2 x 2 track pattern. Often lopes, leaving a C-shaped pattern.

Scat: Varies from pure black animal protein to mostly hair with some bones. Tips tapered into long tails.

Habitat: An animal of the open brush country, the coyote digs its den on exposed hilltops or ridges with a view of surrounding area. Where persecuted, may den in a more secluded location.

Similar species: Even adult track is smaller than that of a wolf pup. Track may overlap in size with red fox, but lacks callus ridge

scat
3.0 x 0.75 in
7.5 x 1.5 cm

SCAT WIDTH

of red fox. Track larger than gray fox, and usually shows claws. Differs from bobcat by showing claws and by having one lobe on leading edge of interdigital pad.

Other sign: Marks territory with urine and scat piles. Scat pile locations may be used repeatedly. Uses feet to scratch near scat piles, spreading odor from scat and foot glands to identify territory.

scratch marks near scat pile

lope

front
2.5 x 2.35 in
6.3 x 5.8 cm

hind
2.25 x 1.9 in
5.7 x 4.8 cm

side trot

Red Wolf
Canis rufus

About German shepherd size, males are 45.0 to 90.0 pounds (20.0 kg to 40.0 kg) and females are 35.0 to 65.0 pounds (16.0 to 30.0 kg). Lankier than a gray wolf, with long legs. Color varies from cinnamon buff to red with gray and black on the back and tip of tail. Underside is white to pinkish.

Track: Track about size of a baseball. Claws usually present; one lobe on leading edge of interdigital pad. Inside toe slightly larger than outside. Front foot larger than hind. Given rarity of red wolves, measurements below are approximate. More data are needed.

Trail: Trotting stride averages 60.0 inches (150.0 cm). Often uses a C-shaped gallop or a trot with the body turned to the side, leaving a 2 x 2 pattern.

Scat: Varies from pure black, toothpaste-like animal protein to mostly hair with some bones. Tips tapered into long tails.

scat
4.0 x 1.25 in
10.0 x 3.2 cm

SCAT WIDTH

Habitat: Found in all habitats. Tends to use cover when possible, moving in forest or at forest-meadow edge.

Similar species: Track larger than other canids. Differs from mountain lion by having one lobe on the leading edge of the interdigital pad and usually showing claws. Differs from bear by having only four toes, with the large toe on the inside.

Other sign: The alpha wolf, dominant member of the pack, marks its territory by urinating on raised objects along the trail. Blood observed during January or February in the female's urine stain may indicate readiness to breed. Scratch marks beside urine stains or scat are territorial markings, and are usually made with hind feet.

side trot

urine mark of
alpha wolf

front
3.5 x 3.0 in
8.8 x 7.5 cm

hind
3.25 x 2.75 in
8.0 x 7.0 cm

gallop

FRONT TRACK LENGTH

FRONT TRACK WIDTH

Bobcat
Lynx (Felis) rufus

Size of a border col-lie, weighing 13.0 to 35.0 pounds (6.0 to 16.0 kg). Males larger than females. Overall color reddish to yellowish brown, with dark spots or streaks and whitish underside. Ears have tufts at tips. Back of ears and top of tail tip black. Tail is short or bobbed, about 4.0 inches (10.0 cm) long.

Track: Front track is round or wider than long. Hind track may be longer than wide. Claw impressions are usually absent. Toes form a slight arc and toe 3 leads. The leading edge of the interdigital pad has two lobes. Inside toe distinctly larger than outside toe.

Trail: Walking stride is about 20.0 inches (50.0 cm). Usually walks, but bounds with hind feet placed side by side when chasing prey. Winter trails often show random vertical leaps, perhaps signaling that the bob-cat has jumped after a flying bird.

Scat: Tends to be constricted and, if dry, separates at constrictions into segments. Ends usually blunt. Dry scat falls apart. Scat from a fresh kill may form a cord of uniform diameter.

broken constriction

scat
3.0 x 0.8 in
7.5 x 2.0 cm

Habitat: Prefers dense cover of swamps and forests, especially with rocky ledges. Open agricultural land is not used. Rock piles, caves, and high rocky ledges are important for bearing young.

Similar species: Differs from coyote and other canids by lacking claws, having two lobes on the leading edge of the interdigital pad, and having toe 3 substantially leading. Substantially smaller than both lion and lynx.

Other sign: Scent marks made by urine, scat, and anal glands. Scrapes dirt or snow over urine and scat. Scratches from rubbing glands are apparent on snow. Caches food by burying.

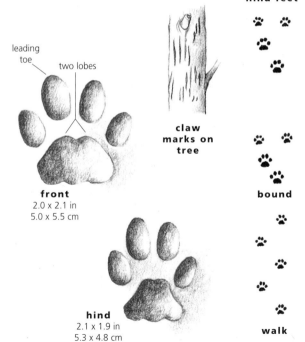

leading toe

two lobes

front
2.0 x 2.1 in
5.0 x 5.5 cm

claw marks on tree

hind
2.1 x 1.9 in
5.3 x 4.8 cm

walk

vertical leap from hind feet

bound

walk

FRONT TRACK LENGTH

FRONT TRACK WIDTH

Mountain Lion
Puma concolor

About the size or larger than an Irish wolfhound, with male averaging 145.0 pounds (66.0 kg) and female about 120.0 pounds (54.0 kg). Color gray to red, often called tawny, with whitish underside. Back of ears and tail tip black to brown. Tail is more than half the length of the body. Also called cougar or puma. May be reestablishing in east or migrating from Florida, track verification needed—photos or casts.

Track: Track diameter of a baseball. Front track round or wider than long, and hind track longer than wide. Claw impressions are usually absent. Toes form a slight arc and toe 3 leads. Leading edge of the interdigital pad has two lobes. Inside toe distinctly larger.

Trail: Walking stride is about 36.0 inches (90.0 cm). Usually walks, but bounds with hind feet placed side by side when chasing prey.

Scat: Scat from a fresh kill may form a cord of uniform diameter with very slight constrictions; ends usually blunt. As the carcass a lion is feeding on dries out, the lion's scat tends to develop constrictions, eventually falling apart when diet becomes dry.

scat
4.0 x 1.25 in
10.0 x 3.1 cm

SCAT WIDTH

Habitat: Habitat is that of its main prey, deer. Open woodlands with rock ledges and grass (for deer) preferred. Often found in riparian zones with trees.

Similar species: Track differs from wolf by the presence of two lobes on the leading edge of the interdigital pad, by having toe 3 substantially leading, and by usually not showing claws. Differs from wolverine and bears by having only four toes and large toe inside.

Other sign: Often buries scat by scraping dirt over it with front feet. Scraped ground material may conceal food caches. Male will rake up football-size patches of brush and urinate on them to mark home range.

Comments: Spreading east and breeding populations not known from area. However, wandering animals may move through. Proof of non-feral or non-escaped breeding in animals is needed.

scraped ground around scat

two lobes

front
3.5 x 3.5 in
8.8 x 9.0 cm

leading toe

hind
3.25 x 3.0 in
8.1 x 7.5 cm

bound

walk

FRONT TRACK LENGTH

FRONT TRACK WIDTH

Black Bear
Ursus americanus

Calf-size bear, female averaging 120.0 pounds (54.0 kg) and male about 300.0 pounds (135.0 kg). Male grows faster and obtains larger size than female. Color varies from black to brown to blond to red.

Track: Claws on front foot, seldom longer than toes, are usually present. Little toe is set back from rest of toes. Hind print has a large, humanlike heel. Outside toe is larger than others.

Trail: Walking stride 35.0 to 40.0 inches (88.0 to 100.0 cm). Usually ambles, a fast walk where the hind foot oversteps the front. Gait is pigeon-toed. Lopes in a C-shaped pattern or a side gallop.

Scat: Normally contains vegetation and is sweet-smelling. When feeding on carcasses, scat varies from black to brown, with mostly hair and some bones. Ants often found in scat. Tips have a short taper or are blunt.

animal protein

scat
7.0 x 1.0 in
17.8 x 2.5 cm

berries

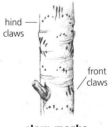

hind claws

front claws

claw marks on tree

SCAT WIDTH

Habitat: Forest, seldom venturing far into wide openings. Thick understory vegetation and abundant food sources are critical.

Similar species: Differs from mountain lion and wolf by having five toes.

Other sign: Claws trees, rips open logs, digs into ant piles, and turns over rocks and scat as it looks for insects.

side lope

lope

faint little toe

big toe

front
4.5 x 4.0 in
11.3 x 10.0 cm

arch

hind
7.0 x 3.5 in
17.8 x 8.8 cm

amble

FRONT TRACK LENGTH

FRONT TRACK WIDTH (50%)

Raccoon
Procyon lotor

The size of a Jack
Russell terrier,
stocky, with broad
head and bushy tail.
Male averages 18.0
pounds (8.0 kg) and
female 16.0 pounds
(7.0 kg). Gray to black overall,
with black rings on the tail and a black mask on a white face.

Track: Five slender toes, slightly bulbous on the ends. Feet resemble small human hands and feet. Hind foot has a long, naked heel.

Trail: Walking stride averages 27.0 inches (68.0 cm). Roll of hips during walk causes hind foot to register beside the opposite front print. C-shaped gallop is common.

Scat: Highly variable, but often black, even-diameter cord with blunt ends. Often contains crayfish or fruit. Deposited singly or in dung heaps containing scat from perhaps several raccoons. **Caution: May carry a parasite that is potentially fatal to humans. Do not smell scat, and wash hands after touching.**

Habitat: River and stream drainages are prime habitats, but storm drains in cities may also provide refuge. Woodpiles in and around towns.

SCAT WIDTH

scat
3.0 x 0.75 in
7.5 x 1.9 cm

Similar species: Differs from bear by having smaller tracks and slender toes. Differs from river otter by lack of webbing. Larger than mink.

Other sign: Digs holes in stream banks to get at crayfish. Leaves piles of crayfish skeletons and claws. Digs for worms in lawns.

sign left while fishing for crayfish

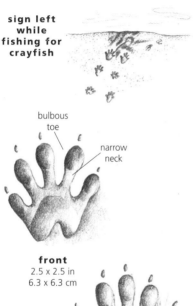

bulbous toe

narrow neck

front
2.5 x 2.5 in
6.3 x 6.3 cm

hind
4.0 x 2.3 in
10.0 x 5.8 cm

gallop

walk

FRONT TRACK LENGTH

FRONT TRACK WIDTH

Weasels
Mustela species

Long-tailed weasel
M. frenata

Three species,
with long, slen-
der bodies, varying in
size from a regular to a
foot-long hot dog. Pointed, flat skull with small ears.
Males up to twice as large as females. Largest males weigh
about 1.0 pound (450.0 g). Overall color is brown, with a
white belly. In winter, northern individuals turn entirely
white. Hairy, slender tail. The small least weasel (*M. nivalis*)
lacks the black tip on the tail found in the ermine
(*M. erminea*) and the long-tailed weasel.

Track: Wide track. Five toes, in 1-3-1
grouping. Little toe, on inside of foot,
often does not register. Interdigital pad
chevron-shaped. Heel seldom shows.
Difficult to distinguish among species.

Trail: Galloping stride varies from 8.0 to
30.0 inches (20.0 to 75.0 cm). Side-by-
side tracks, when examined closely, show
one track slightly in front of the other—a gallop. In snow, a drag
mark may be found between front and hind prints, sometimes
forming a dumbbell shape. The dumbbell shape indicates fast
movement, with hind feet overstepping front tracks.

Scat: Long, slender cord, usually with black, toothpaste-like animal protein or hair. Cord tends to fold back on itself. Tapered at
both ends.

folded back ———

scat
1.5 x 0.1 in
3.5 x 0.3 cm

tail

SCAT WIDTH

Habitat: Prefer dense, low ground cover to open areas. Found in habitats where their prey, rodents, occur in high densities. Trails often lead from one rodent den to another. Travel in snow and ground burrows of other mammals.

Similar species: Differ from other mustelids by their smaller size and the drag mark commonly located between twin track patterns in the snow.

Other sign: Routes seldom follow a straight line, often having many sharp turns. Scat often deposited on raised objects.

erratic route

dumbbell shape

weasel trail

foot drag

gallop

front
0.5 x 0.6 in
1.3 x 1.5 cm

proximal pad

heel not included in track measurement

hind
0.6 x 0.7 in
1.5 x 1.8 cm

2 x 2 lope

FRONT TRACK LENGTH

FRONT TRACK WIDTH

Mink
Mustela vison

Size of a small
domestic cat, but
slender, 1.5 to 3.5
pounds (0.7 to 1.5 kg).
Male 10 percent larger than
female. Pointed, flat skull with
small ears. Overall color is dark brown, with
white spots on chin and chest. Hairy, slender tail.
Webbing occurs between the toes.

Track: Five toes, in 1-3-1 grouping. Little toe, on the inside of foot, sometimes does not register. Webbing shows between toes in tracks; look carefully. Interdigital pad chevron-shaped. Proximal pad may show in front footprint. Heel seldom shows.

Trail: Bounding stride averages 14.0 inches (35.0 cm). Bounds more than weasels, but a gallop, averaging 20.0 inches (50.0 cm), is also common.

Scat: Long, slender cord, usually tending to fold back on itself. Black or brown in color, occasionally with hair. Tapered at both ends. Often contains remains of fish or crayfish. May be oily and smell fishy. Fish oil keeps scat composed of fish scales from falling apart until oil evaporates, then scales scatter on the ground.

tail

folded back

fish bones

scat
2.0 x 0.25 in
5.0 x 0.6 cm

SCAT WIDTH

Habitat: River- and streambanks. Seldom far from water.

Similar species: Differs from other small mustelids by having more webbing between toes. Larger than weasels. Use of aquatic habitat is an important clue for separation from marten. Tracks and trail much smaller than otter's.

Other sign: Mink make "post offices," repeated scat deposits on logs exposed above water's edge. Strong, musky, almost skunklike odor from anal scent glands.

fast walk

web

proximal pad

front
1.7 x 1.8 in
4.3 x 4.5 cm

web

hind
1.8 x 1.9 in
4.5 x 4.8 cm

bound

FRONT TRACK LENGTH

FRONT TRACK WIDTH

Fisher
Martes pennanti

Size of a large
domestic cat,
but slender, 7.5 to
12.0 pounds (3.0 to
5.0 kg). Male larger
than female. Pointed,
flat skull with small ears. Color is dark brown. Long bushy
tail.

Track: Five toes, in 1-3-1 grouping.
Little toe, on the inside of foot, sometimes does not register. Interdigital pad
chevron-shaped. Proximal pad may
show in front footprint. Heel seldom
shows. Claws short. Feet are not well
furred, which, in winter, makes toes
appear clearly in tracks.

Trail: Galloping stride averages 28.0
inches (70.0 cm). Mostly gallops, but walking, 3 x 3, 1 x 2 x 1,
and 4 x 4 gallop patterns are also common.

Scat: Only mustelid scat that frequently contains porcupine quills.
Long, slender cord, usually tending to fold back on itself. Black or
brown in color, occasionally with hair. Tapered at both ends.

Habitat: Old-growth forest, especially among conifers and large
timber, and in swamp areas. Upland hardwood stands where por-
cupines den. Will use young forest stands following fire or timber

folded back

tail

scat
3.5 x 0.5 in
8.8 x 1.3 cm

SCAT WIDTH

harvest. Avoids open areas without overhead cover, but will travel on roads and trails.

Similar species: Lacks the webbed toes of the mink. Differs from mink by habitat and use of terrestrial sites. Larger than mink and marten and occupies areas of shallower snow. Smaller than wolverine and makes more frequent use of trees for walkways and nests.

Other sign: Porcupine skins turned inside out. Snow trails may reveal frequent trips up trees. Walks on logs to avoid deep snow. Drags stomach over objects that protrude from the ground or snow to scent mark, leaving scratches. Travels on packed trails of snowshoe hare.

1 x 2 x 1 lope

proximal pad

front
2.5 x 2.8 in
6.3 x 7.0 cm

hind
2.6 x 2.4 in
6.5 x 6.0 cm

3 x 3 lope

2 x 2 gallop

FRONT TRACK LENGTH

FRONT TRACK WIDTH

River Otter
Lontra (Lutra) canadensis

Body and tail form a
4-foot-long cylinder
that tapers to a hairy,
pointed tail. Weight
varies from 10.0 to 30.0
pounds (5.0 to 14.0 kg).
Male slightly larger than female. Overall
color a rich, dark brown, with silver-brown belly. Webbed
toes on front and hind feet.

Track: Large webbed foot is diagnostic, but look closely because webbing may be difficult to see. Hind foot is very wide. Five toes, in 1-3-1 grouping. Little toe, on the inside of foot, sometimes does not register. Interdigital pad chevron-shaped. Proximal pad often shows. Hairless heel on hind foot.

Trail: Walking stride averages 19.0 inches (48.0 cm). Loping stride averages 32.0 inches (80.0 cm). Loping gait patterns are usually turned to the side. Tail drag often observed.

Scat: Usually contains fish remains, including scales and vertebrae. The texture is oily and the smell fishy.

fish parts —

scat
5.0 x 1.0 in
12.5 x 2.5 cm

Habitat: River- and streambeds. Lives and nests in bank burrows, but may also nest in logjams. In spring, travels overland, often several miles from water sources.

Similar species: Differs from other species by webbing and large, wide hind foot.

Other sign: Loose dirt banks show where otters have rolled to dry off. Rolls around tufts of grass, twisting them into scent posts. Travels by sliding down banks and along level snow and over ice-covered lakes.

tail drag

side lope

webbing

proximal pad

front
2.5 x 3.0 in
6.3 x 7.5 cm

web

hind
3.0 x 3.6 in
7.5 x 9.0 cm

bound

FRONT TRACK LENGTH

FRONT TRACK WIDTH

Spotted Skunk
Spilogale putorius

Black and white, the size of a small domestic cat. Male weighs 1.0 to 2.0 pounds (0.5 to 0.9 kg), female 0.5 to 1.25 pounds (0.25 to 0.6 kg). Distinctive pattern of white spot on forehead, a spot by each ear, three white stripes along each side, and a white tip on tail. Spots and stripes highly variable.

Track: Size of a quarter, with longer claws on front footprint. Five toes, though 1-3-1 grouping is difficult to identify. Little toe, on the inside of foot, may not register. Clear front and hind prints on a hard surface may show a total of six hairless interdigital and proximal pads. Plantigrade heel on hind foot.

Trail: Loping stride is about 12.0 inches (30.0 cm). Short bounds are very common. Often rambles as it walks, leaving a confused trail with most front and hind prints registering separately.

blunt

scat
1.5 x .25 in
3.8 x 0.6 cm

SCAT WIDTH

insect remains

Scat: Cylindrical, with blunt ends. Lacks the long taper and tendency to fold back on itself common in other mustelid scat. May include mouse fur, bird feathers, insects, and carrion.

Habitat: Brush and open woodlands, especially along streams and in boulder areas.

Similar species: Distinguished from striped skunk by smaller track size and second proximal pads. Some authors put skunks in their own family separate from weasels.

Other sign: Nests in burrows beneath rock- and woodpiles or under buildings.

front
0.9 x 1.0 in
2.3 x 2.5 cm

faint pad

heel not included in
track measurement

hind
1.25 x 0.9 in
3.1 x 2.3 cm

lope

side lope

FRONT TRACK LENGTH

FRONT TRACK WIDTH

Striped Skunk
Mephitis mephitis

Black-and-white mustelid, size of a domestic cat, with triangular head. Weight varies from 4.0 to 10.0 pounds (2.0 to 5.0 kg). Male is slightly larger than female. Flat, wide, bushy tail with white hair on top. Long, curved claws for digging.

Track: Half-dollar-size, with long front claws. Hind track looks like a little human footprint. Five toes, in 1-3-1 grouping. Little toe, on the inside of foot, sometimes does not register. Interdigital pad chevron-shaped. Proximal pad often shows. Hairless heel on hind foot.

Trail: Walking stride averages 12.0 inches (30.0 cm). Meanders and stops often when walking, leaving extra footprints in trail. Lope may be turned to the side or straight forward.

Scat: Cylindrical with blunt ends. Lacks the long taper and tendency to fold back on itself common in other mustelid scat. May be composed entirely of insect parts.

Habitat: Not habitat-specific. Lives where burrows, cavities, or tunnels are present, including in and around buildings. Presence

blunt

scat
5.0 x 0.75 in
12.5 x 1.9 cm

fanged puncture

chewed eggs

SCAT WIDTH

of insects and small mammals is critical to habitat selection.

Similar species: Differs from other species by having long, wide claws on the front foot. Smaller than badger, with front and hind feet similar in size. Larger than spotted skunk and has only one proximal pad. Some authors put skunks in their own family seperate from weasels.

Other sign: Smell of skunk musk identifies nests and burrows. Tears apart nests of small mammals. Bird eggs show four fang punctures around larger hole in shell.

1 x 2 x 1 lope

long, wide claws

insect remains

front
1.5 x 1.25 in
3.8 x 3.1 cm

proximal pad

hind
1.9 x 1.4 in
4.8 x 3.5 cm

side lope

FRONT TRACK LENGTH

FRONT TRACK WIDTH

Cottontail Rabbit
Sylvilagus species

Small rabbit with large ears and feet, but small white tail. Averages about 3.0 pounds (1.4 kg). Color pepper-and-salt or gray and white. Two species of cottontail are found in the region. The tracks of these species are indistinguishable from one another.

Eastern Cottontail
Sylvilagus floridanus

Track: Toes asymmetrical around foot axis. Track indistinct because the foot is completely haired and lacks pads. Occasionally claws will register; these may be the only sign of a hopping rabbit. Hind footprint about two and a half times longer than front.

Trail: Hopping stride is about 3.0 feet (90.0 cm). Most of the time rabbits hop, but walking patterns will occasionally be observed.

Scat: Dry scat is a slightly flattened sphere. Produces a black, semiliquid scat that is usually reingested to utilize remaining nutrients.

scat
0.2 in
0.5 cm

chewed branch and bud

SCAT WIDTH

Habitat: Found wherever there is suitable cover and grass for food, including brush-piles, herbaceous and shrubby vegetation, and grasslands. May use dens of other animals for escape cover.

Similar species: Differs from snowshoe hare by having shorter heels and smaller overall size.

Other sign: Sharp incisors cleanly cut herbaceous vegetation at the height of a sitting rabbit, 4.0 to 8.0 inches (10.0 to 20.0 cm). Look for tips of branches with young sprouts chewed off. The cottontail's bed, known as a **form**, is a shallow depression in earth, grass, or snow.

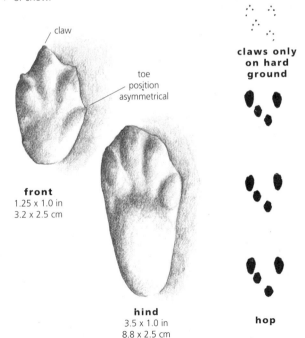

walk

claws only on hard ground

hop

claw

toe position asymmetrical

front
1.25 x 1.0 in
3.2 x 2.5 cm

hind
3.5 x 1.0 in
8.8 x 2.5 cm

FRONT TRACK LENGTH

FRONT TRACK WIDTH

Snowshoe Hare
Lepus americanus

Medium-size hare with
long ears and feet.
Averages about 4.0 pounds
(1.8 kg). Body color is rusty
to gray-brown, turning white
in the winter. Ears retain their
black tip in winter.

Track: Toes asymmetrical around
foot axis. Track indistinct because
the foot is completely haired and lacks
pads. Hind footprint may be up to two
and a half times longer than front. To provide flotation on snow, hind feet are
exceptionally wide and toes may splay
apart so that width approaches length.

Trail: Hopping stride varies from 3.0 to
6.0 feet (0.9 to 1.8 m). Tends to hop with
paired hind feet.

Scat: Dry scat is a slightly flattened sphere. Produces a black,
semiliquid scat that is usually reingested to utilize remaining nutrients.

SCAT WIDTH

scat
0.3 in
0.8 cm

chewed
branch
and cone

Habitat: Mountains with snows. Dense second-growth forest is preferred, but swamps are also used. Forages at forest edge and in small clearings.

Similar species: Track differs from cottontail by its large, wide size.

Other sign: Look for woody plants, including conifers, that have had the tips of branches chewed off. During population highs, hares will strip tree bark and have been observed feeding on carcasses. The snowshoe's nest, a shallow depression known as a form, is found under conifer branches or logs.

toe
position
asymmetrical

front
1.75 x 1.5 in
4.4 x 3.8 cm

hind
4.5 x 3.75 to 4.5 in
11.3 x 9.4 to 11.3 cm

hop

FRONT TRACK LENGTH

FRONT TRACK WIDTH

Woodchuck
Marmota monax

Size of a domestic cat, 5.0 to 10.0 pounds (2.2 to 4.5 kg). Ears and head are short and broad. Tail about one-third body length. Color frosted brown to yellowish brown on back, but paler on belly, dark feet.

Track: Front foot size of a silver dollar, with four toes in 1-2-1 grouping. Five toes on hind foot, 1-3-1 grouping. Toes relatively slender. Four joined interdigital and two proximal pads on front footprint, and four joined interdigital pads on hind foot. Heel is hairless.

Trail: A ground dweller, the woodchuck uses a half bound stride that varies from 15.0 to 40.0 inches (33.0 to 88.0 cm). Walking stride is 18.0 inches (40.0 cm).

Scat: Rare to find because it is deposited in latrines within tunnel systems. Wide variety of forms, from oval pellets to long cords, all of which may be tightly stuck together. Sometimes lacks defined shape, being dark and runny when deposited.

scat
0.25 to 0.5 in
0.6 to 1.3 cm

SCAT WIDTH

Habitat: Open or brushy areas, especially around rocky ravines and cultivated fields.

Similar species: Largest of the squirrels, its track dwarfs other ground squirrels. Track left when drinking at a stream may be distinguished from beaver's by lack of webbing and by having only four toes on front prints.

Other sign: Extensive tunnel system with two or more round-oval openings 5.0 to 7.0 inches (12.5 to 15.0 cm) in diameter. While some openings may have a large mound of dirt, others, excavated to the inside, may not have a mound and be more concealed. Fresh dirt indicates occupancy, if height of burrow exceeds 8.0 inches (18.0 cm), it may have been taken over by red fox.

proximal pad

front
2.2 x 1.8 in
5.5 x 4.5 cm

hind
2.8 x 2.0 in
7.0 x 5.0 cm

bound

FRONT TRACK LENGTH

FRONT TRACK WIDTH

Chipmunk
Tamias striatus

Slightly larger than a large mouse, up to 3.0 ounces (0.08 kg). Reddish fur, with white stripes bordered by black stripes along the sides of the face and body. Haired tail.

Track: Front foot size of a nickel, with four toes in 1-2-1 grouping. Five toes on hind foot, 1-3-1 grouping. Toes relatively slender. Claws short. Hind heel is haired and details are difficult to detect.

Trail: Bounding stride averages 7.0 inches (18.0 cm). Mostly terrestrial, it usually uses a half bound, though full bounds may be observed in its trails.

scat
0.1 in
0.3 cm

SCAT WIDTH

Scat: Small, usually unconnected ovals.

Habitat: Deciduous forest and brush areas.

Similar species: Smaller than ground and tree squirrels. Lacks the long claws of ground squirrel. Smaller than woodchuck.

Other sign: Seeds and nuts of various plants, chewed open on one side.

front
0.5 x 0.4 in
1.3 x 1.0 cm

furred heel, not included in track measurement

hind
0.7 x 0.6 in
1.8 x 1.5 cm

bound

FRONT TRACK LENGTH

FRONT TRACK WIDTH

Red Squirrel
Tamiasciurus hudsonicus

Medium-size squirrel, weighing up to 0.5 pound (0.25 kg). Reddish brown back, separated from white underparts by a black stripe. White ring around eye. Slight ear tufts. Tail is bushy.

Track: Front foot size of a quarter, with four toes in 1-2-1 grouping and five pads. Five toes on hind foot, 1-3-1 grouping and four pads. Toes relatively slender. Claws relatively short. Haired hind heel is indistinct in tracks unless in snow.

Trail: Full bounding stride averages 24.0 inches (60.0 cm). Walk and half bound when searching for food.

Scat: Small, shapeless black masses to small, usually unconnected ovals.

scat
0.1 in
0.3 cm

chewed cones and seed casings

Habitat: Boreal or northern coniferous forests, mixed hardwood forests, and swamps. Infrequently found in deciduous forests.

Similar species: Larger than chipmunk. Lacks the long claws of ground squirrel. Smaller than gray squirrel and woodchuck.

Other sign: Builds twig-and-leaf nests in branches of trees, about 15.0 feet (5.0 m) from the ground. Piles, called middens, of pine and hemlock cone scales where squirrel removes scales to get at seeds. Cones are cached 12.0 inches (30.0 cm) deep in the midden for use as winter food.

hind
prints on
front

slow bound

claws

pads distinct

front
1.2 x 0.75 in
3.0 x 1.9 cm

hind
1.8 x 1.0 in
4.5 x 2.5 cm

full bound

FRONT TRACK LENGTH

FRONT TRACK WIDTH

Eastern Gray Squirrel
Sciurus carolinensis

Large squirrel, weighing up to 1.5 pounds (0.7 kg). Grayish black with some brown in summer. Belly is whitish. Light colored ring around eye. Tail is bushy, bordered with white hairs.

Track: Front foot size of a half-dollar, with four toes in 1-2-1 grouping. Five toes on hind foot, 1-3-1 grouping. Toes relatively slender. Claws relatively short. Haired hind heel is indistinct but may show in tracks especially in snow.

Trail: Bounding stride ranges from 24.0 to 36.0 inches (60.0 to 90.0 cm). Straddle 5.0 inches (12.5 cm). Tends to use a full bound.

Scat: Small, shapeless black masses to small, usually unconnected ovals.

scat
0.25 in
0.6 cm

Habitat: Hardwood forests and river bottoms. Nut producing trees in territory.

Similar species: Larger than chipmunk. Lacks the long claws of ground squirrel. Larger than red squirrel and smaller than woodchuck.

Other sign: Nests in tree holes and builds twig-and-leaf nests in branches of trees, about 25.0 feet (7.6 m) from the ground.

hind
prints on
front

front
1.6 x 1.0 in
4.0 x 2.5 cm

hairless heel

slow bound

hairless heel, not
included in track
measurement

hind
2.6 x 1.4 in
6.5 x 3.5 cm

full bound

FRONT TRACK LENGTH

FRONT TRACK WIDTH

Southern Flying Squirrel
Glaucomys volans

A small squirrel, weighing 4.0 ounces (112.0 g). Its silky fur is olive brown on the back and lead gray on the underside. A fold of skin stretches between front and hind legs and body, forming a wing and allowing the squirrel to glide. Its bushy tail is flattened to aid in sailing.

Track: Front foot size of a quarter, with four toes in 1-2-1 grouping. Five toes on hind foot, 1-3-1 grouping. Toes relatively slender. Claws relatively short and may not show. Hind foot interdigital pads form a tight crescent, proximal pads are lacking.

Trail: Bounding stride averages 20.0 inches (50.0 cm). Uses a full bound.

Scat: Small, usually unconnected ovals.

Habitat: Deciduous and coniferous forests, often found in attics of houses.

scat
0.1 in
0.3 cm

SCAT WIDTH

Similar species: Differs from all other squirrels and chipmunks by the tight crescent of interdigital pads on the hind foot. Lacks the long claws of ground squirrels. Smaller than woodchuck.

Other sign: More active at night. Skin flap outlines may show in dust or snow. Sometimes builds roof on bird nest to use as den. Tree dens may hold twenty squirrels during the winter.

hind prints
on front

wing marks

front
0.5 x 0.5 in
1.3 x 1.3 cm

bound

wing
drag

interdigital pads
arrayed in a
crescent shape

hind
1.5 x 0.5 in
3.8 x 1.3 cm

FRONT TRACK LENGTH

FRONT TRACK WIDTH

White-footed Mouse
Peromyscus leucopus

Small mouse,
weighing up to
1.0 ounce
(28.0 g).
Adults are
reddish brown to
brown on back

with a white belly, juveniles are dark gray on the back with a
light gray belly. Large eyes and ears. Tail is long and haired.
Many species.

Track: Track smaller than a dime. Four
toes on front foot, in 1-2-1 grouping.
Five toes on hind foot, 1-3-1 grouping.
Four joined interdigital and two proximal pads on front footprint, five joined
pads and heel on hind footprint. Heel is
hairless.

Trail: Bounding stride averages 8.0
inches (20.0 cm). Those species that use a full bound are climbers
and nest in grass, shrubs, or trees. Those species that use a half
bound nest on or below ground. Both types occasionally trot. Tail
drag may be present.

scat
0.1 in
0.3 cm

SCAT WIDTH

Scat: Oval-shaped pellets similar to those left by house mice.

Habitat: Ubiquitous, *Peromyscus* are found from deserts to the northern treeline, from below sea level to the top of high peaks.

Similar species: Differs from shrew by having only four toes on the front feet and by being slightly larger. Differs from vole by often showing a tail drag and by most often bounding. Lacks the long heel of the jumping mouse. Smaller than chipmunk.

Other sign: Compact grass nests without entrances may be found under logs, rocks, and boards. Enters and exits through the grass wall, which closes up after passage. Caches large quantities of seeds in any convenient protected area. Leaves feces near and in nest.

tail
drag

4 x 4 bound

front
0.3 x 0.3 in
0.8 x 0.8 cm

remnant pad

hind
0.4 x 0.3 in
1.0 x 0.8 cm

3 x 3 bound

FRONT TRACK LENGTH

FRONT TRACK WIDTH

Allegheny Woodrat
Neotoma magister

Size of a house rat, weighing about 10.0 to 16.0 ounces (280.0 to 454.0 g). Head gray, sides light brown, and

feet and belly white. Densely haired long tail is white below and dark gray above. Back gray to reddish, belly and throat white to light gray. Large naked ears and long whiskers on face.

Track: Four toes with 1-2-1 spacing on front foot and five toes with a 1-3-1 grouping on hind foot. Toes relatively slender, and toe pads slightly constricted. Three joined interdigital, one remnant, and two proximal pads in front footprint and three interdigital palm pads and two proximal pads on hind print.

Trail: Bounding stride is 16.0 inches (40.0 cm) and walking stride is 6.0 inches (15.0 cm). Bounding is probably the most common gait but woodrats also commonly walk.

Scat: Small oval pellets.

scat
0.2 in
0.54 cm

SCAT WIDTH

nest

Habitat: Limestone caves, cliffs, talus slopes, and residual sandstone boulders in beech, poplar, and maple forests. Uses abandoned buildings, especially outhouses.

Similar species: Larger than mice and voles. Differs from squirrels by the presence of heel pads on hind foot.

Other sign: Bulky houses may contain two or more nests. Houses are made from dry grass, shredded bark, fur, feathers, and twigs. Caches of food, including nuts, berries, foliage, and mushrooms, may be found on nest. Nearby "post office" latrines on rocks may be used by several woodrats, creating deep masses of scat, 2.0 inches (5.0 cm) deep.

bound

constricted pad

front
0.7 x 0.6 in
1.8 x 1.5 cm

remnant pad

heel not included in
track measurement

hind
1.5 x 0.9 in
3.8 x 2.3 cm

fast walk

FRONT TRACK LENGTH

FRONT TRACK WIDTH

Voles
Microtus species

Meadow vole
Microtus pennsylvanicus

Many species
of mouse-size
mammals, related
to lemmings and
weighing up to 3.0
ounces (0.08 kg).
Microtus species,
here represented by
the meadow vole, *M. pennsylvanicus*, are gray to gray-brown
on back, with a light colored belly. Small, stocky mammals
with short ears and small eyes, almost hidden by their fur.
Short tails are sparsely haired.

Track: Track smaller than a dime. Four
toes on front foot, in 1-2-1 grouping.
Five toes on hind foot, 1-3-1 grouping.
Four joined interdigital and two proximal pads on front footprint and four
interdigital pads and one proximal on
hind footprint. Heel is hairless.

Trail: Trotting stride 6.0 inches (15.0
cm). Usually trot, seldom bound. Tail usually does not show in the
trail.

Scat: Oval-shaped pellets similar to those left by house mice,
often piled in tennis ball–size latrines that may hold hundreds of
pellets.

scat
0.1 in
0.3 cm

latrine

Habitat: *Microtus* are grass-loving species, found near meadows across North America and north to the Arctic.

Similar species: Differ from shrews by having only four toes on the front feet. Differ from mice by seldom showing a tail drag and by most often trotting. Lack the long heel of the jumping mouse.

Other sign: As snow melts in the spring, grass nests lacking entrances may be found. Snowmelt may also reveal 1.0-inch (2.5-cm) cords of grass and debris, stuffed into snow tunnels during the winter to make space elsewhere in the tunnel network. Vole latrines are usually found near nests, while mice leave feces near and in their nests. Worn runways through the grass.

bound

fast trot

trot

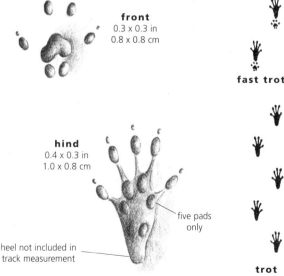

front
0.3 x 0.3 in
0.8 x 0.8 cm

hind
0.4 x 0.3 in
1.0 x 0.8 cm

five pads only

heel not included in track measurement

FRONT TRACK LENGTH

FRONT TRACK WIDTH

Meadow Jumping Mouse
Zapus hudsonius

A small—about 0.8 ounce
(24.0 g)—mouse with long
hind feet and long, sparsely
haired tail. Yellowish sides,
darker brown back,
and white belly.
White tip on long
tail.

Track: Four toes on front foot, in 1-2-1 grouping. Hind foot is about the size of a quarter, has five exceptionally long and narrow toes, in 1-3-1 grouping. Toes relatively slender. Heel is hairless.

Trail: Bounding stride 60.0 to 120.0 inches (150.0 to 300.0 cm). Makes sharp turns during travel. May cover considerable distance per stride when pursued. Tail drag often observed.

scat
0.1 in
0.3 cm

Scat: Small oval pellets.

Habitat: Riparian areas, seldom found more than 3.0 feet (1.0 m) from a stream. Occasionally feeds in meadows.

Similar species: Differs from other rodents in having long, narrow hind feet and tail drag. Differs from kangaroo rat by bounding from all four feet, not just hind.

Other sign: Small piles of grass stems left after eating. Round grass nests.

tail drag

front
0.4 x 0.25 in
1.0 x 0.6 cm

long toes ───

heel not included in track measurement

hind
1.0 x 0.25 in
2.5 x 0.6 cm

bound

FRONT TRACK LENGTH

FRONT TRACK WIDTH

Muskrat
Ondatra zibethica

Large, ratlike, stocky, up
to 4.0 pounds (2.0 kg).
Males slightly larger
than females.
Small eyes and ears.
Tail is black, flattened,
scaly, with few hairs.

Track: Four toes on front foot
(small fifth nubbin may show
in very clear tracks) and five on
hind foot. Toes very slender.
Hind foot appears wider than
long. A fringe of hairs may
show on hind tracks.

Trail: Walking strides average 11.0 inches (28.0 cm). May lope with body turned
to side. Tail drag often visible.

Scat: Oval, at most three to four times
longer than wide. Often deposited in a sticky mass on exposed
logs at water's edge.

Habitat: Marshes and lake edges, secondarily on streambanks.
Large rivers are not as frequently used. Cattails and rushes pre-
dominate.

scat
0.2 in
0.5 cm

SCAT WIDTH

Similar species: Differs from beaver by smaller size and lack of webbing. Differs from mink by long slender toes and by usually walking.

Other sign: Small conical domes made from reeds serve as dens. Cut grass and reeds near water's edge mark feeding sites. Muskrats make "post offices," repeated scat deposits, on rocks.

4 x 4 bound

3 x 3 bound

post office

side lope

front
1.3 x 1.2 in
3.3 x 3.0 cm

fast walk

— wide foot —

toe nubbin

hair fringe

hind
1.3 x 1.6 in
3.3 x 4.0 cm

walk

FRONT TRACK LENGTH

FRONT TRACK WIDTH

American Beaver
Castor canadensis

Largest rodent in North America, 30.0 to 60.0 pounds (14.0 to 27.0 kg). Distinguished by large, webbed hind feet and large, horizontally flattened tail. Fur overall is dark brown to almost black, with lighter belly.

Track: Front and hind prints show five toes. Hind foot may be larger than a human hand. Webbing between hind toes shows, but only when pulled tight by splaying of toes. Clear tracks are difficult to find, as the hind foot steps on the front foot and the dragging tail obliterates many prints.

Trail: Walking stride 18.0 inches (45.0 cm). Tail drag often visible.

Scat: Seldom found, as they are usually deposited in water, where they disintegrate quickly. Marshmallow-size, a little longer than thick. Consist of wood chips.

scat
1.0 x 0.7 in
2.5 x 1.8 cm

SCAT WIDTH

Habitat: Seldom found far from a creek, river, pond, or lake.

Similar species: Differs from other rodents by large size and webbing. Differs from river otter by long, slender toes and pointed heel, and by lacking a chevron-shaped pad.

Other sign: Dams and conical lodges, built of twigs and sticks. Standing, cutoff tree trunks end in a tapered cone. Debarked tree limbs in the water.

lodge

front
3.0 x 2.75 in
7.5 x 7.0 cm

web

hind
5.0 x 5.5 in
12.5 x 13.8 cm

walk

FRONT TRACK LENGTH

FRONT TRACK WIDTH

Porcupine
Erethizon dorsatum

Basketball-size or larger, 10.0 to 25.0 pounds (5.0 to 11.0 kg). Stocky body, with short legs. Distinguished by the presence of quills. Brown to yellowish brown in color.

Track: Rough texture formed by small nubs on soles of feet. Four toes on front foot and five toes on hind. Toes often do not show. Claws often show, especially on front feet.

Trail: Walking stride 17.0 inches (43.0 cm). Tail drag often present.

Scat: Winter scat formed from feeding on conifers is red. Summer scat includes more herbs and shrubs

scat
0.5 in
1.3 cm

debarked stick with chew marks

SCAT WIDTH

and is brown to black. Scat from both seasons may be composed of individual pellets or strings of pellets connected by fibers.

Habitat: Generally found near forests, but may be far from trees if shrubs are available.

Similar species: Rough texture on sole of foot is diagnostic. In snow, trough made by dragging belly highlights its stockiness, separating it from faster-moving mammals.

Other sign: Twigs with bark chewed off, found at the bases of trees. Will perch in a tree for days, chewing the bark, thereby killing the tree.

tail drag

amble

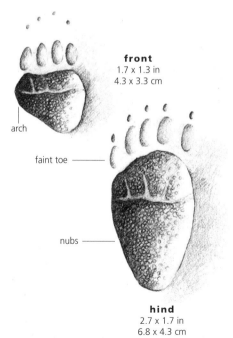

front
1.7 x 1.3 in
4.3 x 3.3 cm

arch

faint toe

nubs

hind
2.7 x 1.7 in
6.8 x 4.3 cm

walk

FRONT TRACK LENGTH

FRONT TRACK WIDTH

Nutria
Myocaster coypus

Muskrat-like rodent weighing 15.0 to 20.0 pounds (6.8 to 9.0 kg). Gray to brown with long, nearly naked round tail. Introduced from South America for fur farming. Escapees are widely distributed.

Track: Four toes on front foot (small fifth nubbin may show in very clear tracks) and five on hind foot. Front print with two interdigital and two proximal pads. Hind print with five interdigital pads and joined proximal pads. Hind foot webbed except between toes 4 and 5. Detached claws.

Trail: Walking stride 12.0 to 14.0 inches (30.0 to 36.0 cm). Occasionally gallops with one measured stride of 18.0 inches (45.0 cm). Walking straddle is 4.0 to 7.0 inches (10.0 to 18.0 cm).

Scat: We have not recorded their scat.

Habitat: Wetlands including marshes, swamps, and lakes.

Similar species: Four toes on front print and five toes on hind print identify as a rodent. Large size and webbing separates it from most other rodents. Lack of webbing between toes 4 and 5 separates it from beaver.

Other sign: Burrows in banks with entrances above water. Nest built in shallow water vegetation.

amble

front
2.1 x 1.6 in
5.3 x 4.0 cm

walk

hind
4.2 x 2.4 in
10.5 x 6.0 cm

slow walk

FRONT TRACK LENGTH

FRONT TRACK WIDTH

White-tailed Deer
Odocoileus virginianus

Smallest member of the deer family. Male averages 130.0 pounds (60.0 kg), female about 110.0 pounds (50.0 kg). Coat is reddish in summer and blue-gray in winter. The prominent white tail is carried erect when animal is disturbed. Antlers, found only on male, have tines, or points, branching off main beam.

Track: Heart-shaped, with convex wall. Pad occupies most of the clout; subunguis slender.

Trail: Walking stride 30.0 inches (75.0 cm). Pronks or stots with front and hind feet striking the ground at the same time. Gallops when in a hurry.

Scat: Usually dry, falls apart when it hits the ground. Pellets vary from nipple-dimple shape to oval.

scat
pellet 0.3 in
pellet 0.8 cm

antler

SCAT WIDTH

Habitat: Generally closed timber, but moves out to grasslands at twilight to feed.

Similar species: Smaller than elk, has more slender tips, and pad occupies most of clout.

Other sign: Gathers (yards up) in large numbers in sheltered groves during the winter. Breaks off limbs of trees when removing the velvet from antlers. Velvet is difficult to find, as both deer and rodents eat the nutrient-rich material. Height of tree wound indicates buck height.

pronk

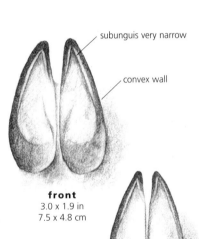

subunguis very narrow

convex wall

front
3.0 x 1.9 in
7.5 x 4.8 cm

hind
2.6 x 1.5 in
6.5 x 3.8 cm

gallop

FRONT TRACK LENGTH

FRONT TRACK WIDTH

Wild Boar / Feral Hog
Sus scrofa

Medium to large-size pig, weights to more than 220.0 pounds (100.0 kg). Boars show great variability as they may be a mixture of European wild boars, recent domestic hogs, and feral hogs. Colors may be black; black and brown; or white, brown, and roan. Hair is coarse and dense. Distribution is expanding and distribution map shows those states where boars are known to exist.

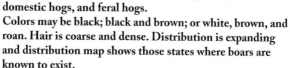

Track: Deer-size tracks. Clouts are rounded and blunt at the tip. Hooves tend to splay. Dewclaws are more pointed and register up to 0.5 inch (1.3 cm) outside and up to 2.0 inches (5.0 cm) behind the hooves.

Trail: Walking stride is 25.0 inches (65.0 cm). Trotting stride is about 55.0 inches (140.0 cm).

soft

scat
pellet 0.4 in
pellet 1.0 cm

firm

SCAT WIDTH

Scat: Seasonally varies from formless on wet, spring diet to pellets to clumps of pellets on dry diets. Diameter of clumps of pellets may be over 2.0 inches (5.0 cm).

Habitat: Scattered distribution in swamps, marshes, and bottom land with mixed deciduous forests. Dense understory and moist soft soil is preferred. Raised dry areas for nests.

Similar species: Differs from deer by their blunt, rounded clouts, greater splay, and widely spaced dewclaws.

Other sign: Boars root up the earth and wallow. Trees are rubbed up to 36.0 inches (90.0 cm) above the ground. Nests are shallow depressions in dry ground occasionally lined with vegetation. Range is expanding.

walk

front
2.5 x 2.1 in
6.3 x 5.3 cm

wide dewclaws

hind
2.1 x 1.8 in
5.3 x 4.5 cm

trot

FRONT TRACK LENGTH

FRONT TRACK WIDTH

Selected reading

Tracks and tracking

Bang, P. et al. 1972. *Collins Guide to Animal Tracks and Signs.* London: Collins Sons.

Brown, R., J. Ferguson, M. Lawrence, and D. Lees. 1987. *Tracks and Signs of the Birds of Britain and Europe: An Identification Guide.* Kent, England: Christopher Helm.

Elbroch, M. 2003. *Mammal Tracks and Sign: A Guide to North American Species.* Mechanicsburg, PA: Stackpole Books.

———. 2001. *Bird Tracks and Sign: A Guide to North American Species.* Mechanicsburg, PA: Stackpole Books.

Fjelline, D. P., and T. M. Mansfield. 1989. Method to Standardize the Procedure for Measuring Mmountain Lion Tracks. In *Proceedings of the Third Mountain Lion Workshop,* ed. R. H. Smith, 49–51. Prescott, AZ: Arizona Game and Fish Department.

Halfpenny, J. C., 2018. *Rare Mammal Moments of the Greater Yellowstone Ecosystem.* A Naturalist's World.

———. 2012. *Charting Yellowstone Wolves.* A Naturalist's World.

———. 2010. *Tracking Wolves: The Basics.* A Naturalist's World.

———, et al. 2009. *Track Plates for Mammals: A How to Manual and Aid to Footprint Identification.* A Naturalist's World.

———. 1997. *Tracking: Mastering the Basics.* 180 min. A Naturalist's World. Videocassette.

———, et al. 1996. "Snow tracking." In *American Marten, Fisher, Lynx, and Wolverines: Survey Methods for Their Detection,* eds. W. Zielinski and T. Kucera, 91–163. General Technical Report PSW-GTR-157. Berkeley, CA: USDA Forest Service, Pacific Southwest Research Station.

———. 1986a. *A Field Guide to Mammal Tracking in North America.* Boulder, CO: Johnson Books.

———. 1986b. *Tracks and Tracking: A How to Guide.* Gardiner, MT: A Naturalist's World. Slides.

Headstrom, R. 1971. *Identifying Animal Tracks: Mammals, Birds, and Other Animals of the Eastern United States.* New York: Dover.

Murie, O. 1954. *A Field Guide to Animal Tracks.* Peterson Field Guide Series. No. 9. Boston: Houghton Mifflin.

Rezendes, P. 1999. *Tracking and the Art of Seeing: How to Read Animal Tracks and Sign.* 2nd ed. Charlotte, VT: Camden House.

Seton, E. T. 1958. *Animal Tracks and Hunter Signs.* New York: Doubleday.

Recommended field identification guides

Burt, W. H., and R. P. Grossenheider. 1964. *A Field Guide to the Mammals.* Peterson Field Guide Series. No. 5. Boston: Houghton Mifflin.

Conant, R. 1958. *Reptiles and Amphibians of Eastern and Central North America.* Peterson Field Guide Series. No. 12. Boston: Houghton Mifflin.

Gosner, K. L. 1985. *Atlantic Seashore.* Norwalk, CT: The Easton Press.

Hamilton Jr., W. J., and J. O. Whitaker. 1979. *Mammals of the Eastern United States.* 2nd ed. Ithaca, NY: Cornell University Press.

Kays, R. W., and D. E. Wilson. 2002. *Mammals of North America.* Princeton, NJ: Princeton University Press.

National Geographic Society. 1983. *Field Guide to the Birds of North America.* Washington, DC: National Geographic Society.

Peterson, R. T. 1984. *Birds of the Eastern United States.* Norwalk, CT: The Easton Press.

Robbins, Chandlers S., B. Bruun, and H. S. Zim. 1983. *A Guide to Field Identification: Birds of North America.* New York: Golden.

Sibley, D. A. 2000. *The Sibley Guide to Birds.* New York: National Audubon Society.

Index

About the authors

James Halfpenny has searched for dinosaur tracks in Colorado and Montana, tracked wildlife in Tanzania and Kenya, studied endangered species on China's Tibet-Qinghai plateau, and researched the polar bears of Hudson Bay and Greenland. Jim specializes in educational, environmentally oriented programs about mammal behavior, tracking, and cold. Since 1961 he has taught outdoor and environmental education for a vast array of schools and organizations, including the Smithsonian, National Outdoor Leadership School, Outward Bound, the Appalachian Mountain Club, The Wilderness Society, National Wildlife Federation, Defenders of Wildlife, and National Audubon Society. He has trained rangers in tracking techniques at Yellowstone, Glacier, Grand Teton, and Rocky Mountain national parks. His research has also taken him to Antarctica, Africa, and Japan, and all over North America. He is a fellow of the Explorers Club and a Vietnam veteran. Halfpenny was featured, with Australian aborigines, Kalahari Bushmen, and Alaskan Inuit, in a documentary about the loss of native tracking skills shown on the Discovery Channel. He is a past field director for the Long-Term Ecological Research program in the Alpine Tundra and project coordinator for the University of Colorado's Institute of Arctic and Alpine Research. He is also the senior author of the *Scats and Tracks* series, *A Field Guide to Mammal Tracking in North America*, *Yellowstone Wolves in the Wild*, *Yellowstone Bears in the Wild*, *Discovering Yellowstone Wolves: Watcher's Guide*, *Charting Yellowstone Wolves*, *Rare Moments of the Greater Yellowstone Ecosystem*, *Track Plates for Mammals*, and *Winter: an Ecological Handbook*. He lives just outside Yellowstone National Park in Gardiner, Montana.

Jim Bruchac was born and raised in the foothills of the Adirondacks. Jim is a professional storyteller, author, and licensed New York State wilderness guide. Jim's first interest in animal tracking came from his father, Dr. Joseph Bruchac III, co-author of the *Keepers of the Earth* series. Other influences include his late grandfather, Joseph Bruchac Jr., "The Adirondack Taxidermist," noted outdoorsman, and member of the Taxidermy Hall of Fame; as well as his continued work with John Stokes, founder of the Tracking Project. Since his first introduction to James Halfpenny in 1996, the two have spent hundreds of hours tracking together. Jim is a member of the International Society of Professional Trackers. Over the years he has offered numerous animal-tracking programs for schools and organizations, including the National Wildlife Federation, New York State Parks, Cornell Outdoor Education, the National Park Service, The Nature Conservancy, and the Environmental Education Council of Ohio. He is also author of numerous books on Native American folklore: *When the Chenoo Howls, Native Tales of Terror, Native American Games and Stories, How Chipmunk Got Its Stripes*, and *At Home on the Earth*. Jim co-authored *Scats and Tracks of the Northeast* and *Scats and Tracks of the Southeast* with James Halfpenny. Jim has been featured as both a storyteller and tracker on several PBS specials as well as the Outdoor Life Network's show, *25 Hardest Animals to Hunt*. Due to their combined efforts in educating others about the natural world, Jim and his father were awarded a 2004 conservation Achievement Award from the National Wildlife Federation. Jim lives in Greenfield Center, New York.

About the illustrator

Todd Telander is a freelance natural science illustrator and wildlife artist. He studied biology and environmental studies at the University of California, Santa Cruz, where he became interested in illustration. His work appears in Falcon's *America's 100 Most Wanted Birds, Birder's Dictionary, A Field Guide to Cows,* and *A Field Guide to Pigs,* as well as in museums, galleries, and private collections. Todd lives in Walla Walla, Washington, with his wife, Kirsten, a writer, and their two sons, Miles and Oliver.